Uncluttered FAITH

How a Professional Skeptic Came to Believe in God

John Scott

Brown Books Publishing Group
Dallas, Texas

Uncluttered Faith
How a Professional Skeptic Came to Believe in God

Brown Books Publishing Group
16250 Knoll Trail Drive, Suite 205
Dallas, Texas 75248
www.BrownBooksSmallPress.com
(972) 381-0009

A New Era in Publishing™

ISBN 978-1-61254-008-5
Library of Congress Control Number 2012930186

1. Faith 2. Apologetics 3. Skepticism 4. Christianity 5. Charity

Printing in the United States
10 9 8 7 6 5 4 3 2 1

Special quantity discounts are available for bulk purchases of this book. Promotional copies are available. For details, contact the publisher.

For more information, please visit: www.UnclutteredFaith.com

Disclaimers

"Frankly, most books 'defending God' almost persuade me to become an atheist. But John Scott's carefully balanced—even respectful—yet penetrating critiques of the convoluted arguments of the 'professional atheists' will be a bright revelation to searchers everywhere."

—Clyde Fant
Author and professor emeritus of religious studies
Stetson University

"This is a book for a layperson. It avoids religious jargon and deals with the issue of faith in a way that an average person can easily understand. I strongly commend John Scott, and I recommend his book to any person who is struggling with their faith. This writing is a valuable contribution to an issue that confronts millions of people."

—Millard Fuller
Co-founder with wife, Linda, of Habitat for Humanity

"John Scott wields logic much like a plastic surgeon uses a scalpel to correct malformations and reduce scars. Well documented, engagingly written, and never condescending, the book also reveals a Christian who really does 'walk the talk.'"

—Kathleen Davis Niendorff
Publishing consultant, literary agent

Praise for *Uncluttered Faith*

"John Scott is a modern C. S. Lewis. Regardless of all other books you may have read about the God debate, your consideration will be incomplete if you fail to read this one. Many people denounce atheists and condemn them. Contrary to such antagonism, former unbeliever John Scott's book is full of empathy. It offers insight and an invitation for atheists who are honest enough to take another look. He shares the journey he took to find that God exists, and he invites others to try the experiment that led him to a leap of faith. I commend his book to you without reservation."

—**Johnnie Godwin**
Author and former president
Evangelical Christian Publishers Outreach

"Even from my perspective as an atheist, I found Scott's book to be extremely thoughtful and well written. He makes many distinctive points worth considering. The most powerful part is the last letter, wherein he challenges the 'Professor' on moral grounds. All other things being equal, more religion implies more charity; less religion, less charity."

—**Bruce Sheiman**
Author of *An Atheist Defends Religion*

"John Scott's book is lucid, engaging, and persuasive. The material is profound, compelling, theologically sound, beautifully simple, closely reasoned, and perfectly clear. Only a man of sterling natural gifts and high intellectual caliber touched by the miracle of God's grace could have written such an account."

—**Foy Valentine**
Author and scholar
Once recognized by *Christian Century* magazine as one of the twenty innovative leaders in the religious world

"With his remarkably fresh approach, retired lawyer and former unbeliever John Scott boldly takes on none other than the world's leading atheist, Richard Dawkins, by systematically exposing the many "flies in his atheistic soup." Scott's strategy is intelligent yet uncluttered, making this a highly readable and thought-provoking book for the honestly searching layman. I heartily recommend that you read this book and try Scott's faith experiment. Why not? You have nothing to lose and everything to gain."

—Barbara Baughman Johnson
Certified life coach, *Dallas Morning News* "Voices" columnist

"*Uncluttered Faith* by John Scott is a must-read for anyone who has ever questioned the existence of God, anyone who has ever struggled with questions of how a good God could allow innocents to suffer in a merciless world, anyone whose faith in God has been battered by religious hypocrisy, anyone who is looking for answers to questions like these that we all ask— or should ask—believers and nonbelievers alike. In this brief, accessible, and entertaining book, Scott shares his own sincere search for truth, respectfully addressing the concerns of those still on the journey. Scott's boldest move, and the one that sets apart from other books like it, is his offer of a practical, step-by-step experiment of faith that will give seekers the answers they are looking for through experience rather than theory and polemics. I recommend this book to atheists, agnostics, and believers who are looking for more than another rehash of theoretical wrangling about God's existence. Anyone looking for real answers for himself or to share with others will find Scott's book invaluable."

—Rebecca Dark
Professor of English literature
Dallas Baptist University

This book is dedicated to
my wife, Joanie, and our son, John.

Contents

Introduction: Back to Basics xiii

Seven Letters to an Atheist

Letter No. 1: Regarding Religion 1

Letter No. 2: Regarding God 35

Letter No. 3: Regarding Experiments 79

Letter No. 4: Regarding Evidence 105

Letter No. 5: Regarding Christianity 115

Letter No. 6: Regarding Doctrines 129

Letter No. 7: Regarding Purpose 149

Acknowledgments 159

Endnotes 161

About the Author

Uncluttered
FAITH

Introduction

Back to Basics

Winston Churchill said, "Men occasionally stumble over the truth, but most pick themselves up and hurry off as if nothing had happened."

That's what I did while looking for reasons to believe in God.

I began reading books on the God debate over fifty years ago. Some were so dense with unfathomable philosophic jargon that they left me muttering, "If this is the way to find the answer, God is only going to be available to a few intellectuals."

Many books today make arguments based on science. Some highly respected scholars, including some former atheists, have concluded that scientific evidence proves the existence of an infinitely intelligent Mind. But some others don't agree. To weigh all their arguments you have to know a lot about multiple fields of science, including astronomy, astrophysics, biology, chemistry, and geology, just to name a few. One famous atheist finally accepted the existence of

God based on the characteristics of deoxyribonucleic acid (DNA).

I just don't have sufficient expertise in all those areas to verify and adjudicate all their conflicting claims. That puts me in an exceedingly large majority—over 99 percent of the world's population. My last diploma has "Doctor" in it, but it relates to law, not science. And less than 1 percent of the people on this planet have a college degree in any field of science, much less all those involved in the God debate.

So where does that leave the rest of us, the more than 99 percent who are not scholars in multiple fields of science? Isn't there a way for us to find the answer?

Yes.

Scattered like gold nuggets throughout some of the books I read were a handful of uncomplicated truths that pointed to the answer. Those truths have led both scientists and nonscientists to put their faith in God—and you don't need a PhD to understand them. They would have been just as clear to me when I was a teenager working in the Texas oil fields. Thank God I finally did focus on them, as they led to an unshakable faith that profoundly changed my life.

This book zooms in on those few basic truths that prevail against all arguments for atheism.

I have written the book in the form of seven letters to the famous atheist Richard Dawkins. Some years ago I might have written them to Antony Flew, a scholar in England. He was regarded as the world's intellectual champion of atheism for more than fifty years. Then, in 2004, he surprised the world by disclosing that he had changed his mind. In fact, he said the evidence for God is "compelling and irrefutable."[1]

As if panicked by that news, several professional atheists soon wrote books defending their ground. Three became surprise No. 1 best sellers:

- *The God Delusion* by Richard Dawkins, a zoologist at Oxford University who has become a virtual evangelist for atheism.
- *God Is Not Great* by Christopher Hitchens, a British writer who made a career of arguing for a variety of unpopular positions.
- *The End of Faith* by Sam Harris, who was a graduate student when he wrote this book.

Other atheists joined the parade, but they make essentially the same arguments as Dawkins, Hitchens, and Harris.

Some scholars believe this new wave of atheism will prove to be a passing fad, like communism in Hollywood during the 1930s and 1940s. But others fear the US will become like much of Europe, where atheism is the prevailing view. In any case, these new advocates for atheism have found a large audience. So I've written this book to point out surprisingly obvious flaws in their arguments.

I've chosen to respond to Richard Dawkins instead of the others for three reasons. First, he came to be regarded as the world's leading atheist after Antony Flew relinquished that "honor." Second, Dawkins made the same arguments as Hitchens and Harris, plus a few more, so by responding to him, I am effectively responding to them as well. Third, the book by Dawkins, *The God Delusion*, is more likely than the others to persuade doubters to choose atheism. Hitchens and Harris mainly preach to their own choirs.

I once met Christopher Hitchens, the author of *God Is Not Great,* in person. He was likable, but when he rose to speak, he reminded me of the religious demagogues he denounced. He made dogmatic pronouncements as if they must be true because he said so forcefully. He did much the same in his book. He declared, for example, that "monotheistic religion is a plagiarism of a plagiarism of a hearsay of a hearsay, of an illusion of an illusion, extending all the way back to a fabrication of a few nonevents."[2] Reconstructing such clever prose into coherent points can be like putting together a jigsaw puzzle only to discover many pieces are missing.

Sam Harris, in *The End of Faith,* was even more verbose than Hitchens, but not nearly so entertaining. I suspect that most who bought his book will never finish it. I forced myself to read it all, but felt a recurring urge to shout, "Spit it out! Get to the point!" Even he acknowledges after more than two hundred pages, "Inevitably, the foregoing will strike certain readers as a confusing eruption of speculative philosophy."[3] More than a hundred pages later he finally arrives at his last note. I will quote it here, but only to give you a taste of his writing: "Whether mysticism entails the transcendence of all concepts is surely an open question. The claim here is merely that the concepts that underwrite our dualistic perception of the world are left aside by mystics."[4] (I have no idea how that is supposed to contribute to the God debate.)

As I said, one reason I've chosen to respond to Richard Dawkins is that he is more persuasive than the others.

But his book also has major problems.[5] A review in the *New York Times*, a publication certainly not known for a pro-religion bias, said parts of his book are "intellectually dishonest" and "the tone is smug and the logic occasionally sloppy."[6] Those flaws show up in Dawkins's comments about a classic argument for faith called "Pascal's Wager." Dawkins's criticism of that argument seems reasonable unless the reader happens to know what Pascal really said. Pascal said the exact opposite of what Dawkins intimates on some key points. But Dawkins isn't the only one to misstate Pascal's Wager. Every book by an atheist that I've read distorts it, ignores it, or like Hitchens and Harris, dismisses it with flippant one-liners devoid of any substance. I'll say more about Pascal's Wager in one of the letters to Dawkins.

Of course the letters you are about to read are not actually private letters that I sent to him and then made public in this book. I just felt that writing as if I were penning personal letters *to* him instead of critical essays *about* him would serve as a constant reminder to practice civility—something that gets sacrificed all too often these days when opposing views are being presented. I do intend to send a courtesy copy of this book to Professor Dawkins with the sincere hope that he will reconsider his position. You may think that's a far-fetched goal. After all, he is deeply invested in atheism, both emotionally and financially. But we could have said that about Antony Flew, and he came to believe in God.

That explains why my book is in the form of letters to Richard Dawkins. Now let me explain why I've had the audacity to write it even though I've never been to a seminary, except as a guest. A friend who had been a seminary professor urged me to write a book like this because I'm *not* a theologian or member of the clergy. He said many doubters, disbelievers, and other skeptics won't read a book by someone in a paid profession that requires them to believe in God. They are more likely to listen to a layman who came from where they are. With a smile, he added that they should identify with me because I'm a "professional skeptic." I've been called that a lot, mostly because I'm a lawyer. I feel obliged to be a skeptic because no client wants to be represented by a gullible attorney.

I practiced law for forty years, then retired and became an adjunct university professor teaching a course in leadership. Both careers required analytical thinking and writing on a variety of subjects. However, the experiences that led to this book began while I was in high school in Midland, Texas. I became a church-going Christian while dating a preacher's daughter. I played football and ran the mile on the track team, but religion became more important to me than sports. Then I joined the debate team and enjoyed some success at that. One reason for that success was my willingness to see both sides of an issue. That may be one reason I later struggled with doubts about God.

My teenage love affair with religion waned a bit due to some mixed messages from a visiting evangelist. My impression of what he said can be summed up with these lines from the songwriter Butch Hancock about another town in west Texas: "Life in Lubbock, Texas, taught me two things: One is that God loves you and you're going to burn in hell. The other is that sex is the most awful, filthy thing on earth and you should save it for someone you love."

My doubts about religion and God were amplified in college. I tried to silence them by reading more books arguing for God's existence. But I was also exposed to more arguments on the other side, and I developed strong negative feelings about some arrogant and self-righteous religious classmates. In retrospect I can see that my doubts were based more on emotional reactions to religious people than on intellectual reasons to reject God.

For a time I tried to push doubts about God out of my thoughts, but they kept gnawing at my faith like termites until it collapsed. However, my lack of faith was even more riddled with doubts than my faith had been. So I kept reading everything I could get my hands on about the issue.

After reading countless books, I felt sure I'd seen the crux of every argument ever made on both sides. But in recent years a new argument has emerged. It's based on the characteristics of deoxyribonucleic acid, often referred to by its abbreviation: DNA. It would be more accurate to say it's based on DNA and RNA, the latter standing for ribonucleic acid. Their molecules contain, transmit, and activate extraordinary amounts of genetic information that produce life, including every cell in your body and mine. They tell some to form an eye, some a brain, others a heart, and so forth. Some scientists say the only plausible explanation for DNA and RNA is an infinitely intelligent Mind.[7] That is the main reason the atheist Antony Flew changed his mind and came to believe in God.

I am impressed by what little I understand about the arguments based on those two acids—but most of what I've looked up about them looks like ancient hieroglyphics to me. Therefore I remain grateful to have found the uncomplicated path described in this book. To follow it you don't have to acquire a vast knowledge of science, but you don't have to reject any findings of science, either. Scientists and nonscientists alike, including former atheists and agnostics, can be seen side by side on that path. And it doesn't have a lot of detours into secondary doctrinal disputes. It leads straight to an uncluttered faith that can profoundly change your life.

Whether you are searching for your own answer to the God question or a way to help others, I hope reading this book will be a helpful and enjoyable experience for you.

Letter No. 1

Regarding Religion

Dear Professor Dawkins:
This letter concerns your book *The God Delusion*. You've
said it has drawn some angry responses. This is not going
to be one of those. I have no right to be angry with you, as
I once felt the same way you do about God and religion—I
still feel that way about some religion.

However, I can understand why some folks get angry
with you. While practicing law I observed countless
examples of something I learned from studying psychology:
anger can be caused by fear. Many parents of college
students fear you will persuade their children to jettison
religion—and their morals along with it. That can have
devastating consequences at that critical stage in their lives.
As a lawyer, and now as a professor, I've seen that happen.
So it's easy to see why some otherwise loving people loathe
you, just as they despise those who try to sell illegal drugs
to their kids. I'm not saying they should feel that way, but
I can see why they do. They just don't see any virtuous
motives for what you're doing.

Nevertheless, I will not join the chorus of those who demonize you. I don't share their view that all atheists are evil. I've done volunteer work with an atheist for an organization that helps people with disabilities. He does enough of that sort of thing to put many religious people to shame. And I once read a letter from an atheist who goes to Christmas Mass with his grandmother because, as he said, "What harm is there in attending a church service to make a loved one happy?" So I believe individual atheists can be just as kind and considerate as anyone. Statistical studies show that people of faith are far more likely to be charitable than atheists, but the ratio is not one hundred to zero.

From what I've seen of you on TV and the Internet, I suspect you're a decent fellow, Professor. I saw you remain polite when a famous TV host was rude to you. On the other hand, I've seen you be a bit rude yourself. During the Q&A following one of your college lectures, a student asked, "What if you are wrong?" That was an important question and she asked it in a respectful way. But instead of giving an answer, you ridiculed her for asking it, provoking other students to laugh at her. I didn't admire you for that, but nobody's perfect and I've done worse things myself.

> I will not presume to point out any flaws in your character, but I will respectfully point out flaws in your arguments.

In any event, the God you say doesn't exist has not appointed me to be your judge. Therefore I will not presume to point out any flaws in your character, but I will respectfully point out flaws in your arguments.

Since you began your book by attacking religion, I will respond to that first. In my next letter, I will contest your arguments against God.

Imagine No Religion

On the first page of your book, you invite the reader to "imagine, with John Lennon, a world with no religion." Of course you're referring to a line in his popular song "Imagine" from the 1970s. You follow that with a few lines of your own: "Imagine no suicide bombers, no 9/11," and you continue with a list of bad things done by religious extremists.[8]

Imagine a World with No Atheism

To be fair, Professor, imagine a world in which there has never been any atheists. Imagine no Joseph Stalin, who deliberately caused the deaths of 20–30 million of his own citizens during peacetime in the Soviet Union. Imagine no Mao Zedong, who was responsible for the deaths of an estimated 70–100 million of his own countrymen in China. Imagine no Pol Pot, who eliminated approximately 20 percent of the Cambodian population. If you add the victims of Lenin, Khrushchev, Brezhnev, and other avowed atheists, the total climbs far above 100 million.[9]

According to some estimates, that's more than ten times all the victims of religious extremists throughout all of history, both in terms of absolute numbers and as percentages of the world's population at the times such killings occurred. That is true even if you use maximum— and almost certainly exaggerated—estimates for killings during the Crusades, the Spanish Inquisition, and other atrocities attributed to religious motives.[10]

In an effort to narrow that gap, some atheists say religion has been the cause of most military conflicts. That claim is usually made without supporting data, as if it were general knowledge. Ironically, it has been shown to be false by an atheist, Bruce Sheiman. Using verified facts, not visceral feelings, he debunks the myth that most wars have been waged with religious motives. His book, *An Atheist Defends Religion*, is based on an analysis of hundreds of published studies. Referring to one of those studies, Sheiman says, "Revealingly, in his *Encyclopedia of Wars*, Charles Phillips chronicled a total of 1,763 conflicts throughout history, of which just 123 were categorized as religious. And it is important to note that over the last century the most brutality has been perpetrated by nonreligious cults."[11] Even some conflicts between religious groups have had nonreligious causes, such as the economic and political tensions between Catholics and Protestants in Northern Ireland.

As a lawyer, I have been amused by the hypocrisy of some American atheists on this point. They cite the United States as an example of a "Christian nation" that has gone to war. But then they turn around and allege that the US is *not* a Christian nation in lawsuits to remove the word "God" and the cross from public property.

That said, however, I believe it is a waste of time to argue over how many more people have been murdered by atheists than by religious extremists. Even if bad religion is the lesser evil, that doesn't prove God exists. Nor would the reverse of that prove God doesn't exist. And I will offer a positive case for good religion soon enough in this letter.

In short, Professor, one can agree with your criticisms of religious extremists and still believe in God. Jesus himself called some of the most religious people in his community hypocrites, fools, sons of hell, blind guides, snakes, greedy, self-indulgent, and a den of robbers.[12] I suspect he would say much the same about more than a few of his ostensible followers today.

What is the Cure for Evil Religion?

Jesus taught that the remedy for bad religion is one based on love and the Golden Rule. Your solution would be to get rid of *all* religion, which would be like curing a headache with a guillotine.

> Jesus taught that the remedy for bad religion is one based on love and the Golden Rule.

How would you feel if we applied your reasoning to science?

Since you're a professor of science, I assume you've read the book *When Science Goes Wrong* by Simon LeVay. The author has impressive credentials and has served on the faculties of Harvard Medical School and the Salk Institute. He says that "for every brilliant scientific success there are a dozen failures," and often "science doesn't just fail—it goes spectacularly, even horribly wrong."[13] His book gives some horrifying examples from the "dark side" of scientific discoveries. There have been millions more. For example, scientists found hundreds of uses for asbestos. It remained in wide use for decades until it was found to cause malignant mesothelioma. Many medically approved drugs have caused birth defects and death, not to mention those caused by nuclear accidents. Virtually every day we hear about tragedies caused by science.

Not all horrific results of science have been unintended. Scientists invented chemical and bacterial weapons used for mass murders. Unspeakable experiments were performed on prisoners in the Nazi concentration camps.

The term "mad scientist" is not limited to science fiction.

Now, Professor, what would you think if someone proposed a ban on scientific experiments to avoid the risk of more tragedies? What would you say if they opposed the teaching of science in schools?

You would probably call that insane thinking. Well, that's how I feel when you talk about the worst of religion and remain stone silent about the best. Some forms of religion are to religion what pseudoscience is to science.

Science and religion will doubtless lead to more bad science and bad religion. But let's not throw out either baby with the bathwater just to avoid having more bathwater to throw out later.

You sometimes talk as if an evil person's belief in God proves there is no God. That would be like saying a mad scientist's belief in subatomic particles proves there's no such thing. Sir Isaac Newton was an extremely unpleasant man, but possibly the greatest scientist in history.

The absence of all religion would have cataclysmic consequences, even for atheists.

I suppose this letter on religion could end on that note. Bad things done by religious people don't prove there is no God. So I *could* move on to my next letter and explain how I came to believe in God.

However, I don't want to leave your negative comments about religion unchallenged. I believe the absence of all religion would have cataclysmic consequences, even for atheists.

Go Back to Your Starting Point

Let's continue something you stopped prematurely, Professor: imagining a world with no religion. All you did was imagine a world with no *bad* religion. But what about a world with no good religion, either?

Imagine a world without all the medical institutions—including hospitals, research facilities, and medical, nursing, and dental schools—built by Catholics, Baptists, Jews, Lutherans, Methodists, Anglicans, Mormons, and Presbyterians. The famous St. Jude Children's Research Hospital would not exist. Neither would any of the institutions in the world-class Baylor Health Care System, which began with a single hospital in 1903 when its cofounder, the Baptist minister Dr. George W. Truett, said, "Is it now time to build a great humanitarian hospital, one to which men of all creeds and those of none may come with equal confidence."

Imagine no Catholic Relief Services that provide humanitarian assistance to sixty million people around the world each year.

Imagine no Salvation Army. In 2006, the year in which your book was published, Professor, and just in the

US, the Salvation Army provided humanitarian services to 31,299,690 people by serving 63,797,875 meals; supplying clothes, furniture, and gifts to 22,137,386 people; and providing lodging to 10,738,082 people. These figures are just for one year in the US, which is only one of more than one hundred countries in which the Salvation Army serves. Peter Drucker, the great management expert, said the Salvation Army is "by far the most effective organization in the United States. No one even comes close to it in respect to clarity of mission, ability to innovate, measurable results, dedication, and putting money to maximum use."[14]

Imagine no Habitat for Humanity. By the end of the year in which your book was published, Habitat had built affordable houses for more than one million people in three thousand communities in the US, India, and other lands. Although founded as a Christian organization, Habitat also builds houses for people of other faiths and for those of none.

Imagine a world without Operation Smile, founded by Dr. William Magee and his wife, Kathleen. They are Catholics. He is a plastic surgeon and she is a nurse. They invited other plastic surgeons and nurses to volunteer and perform corrective and reconstructive facial surgeries, mostly on children. Operation Smile led to another organization called Smile Train, which specializes in cleft surgeries and training local doctors.

By the end of the year in which your book was published, Operation Smile and Smile Train had operated on hundreds of thousands of children around the world. Many of those kids had been hiding, ashamed to be seen in public. Now they love to be seen and to smile at themselves in the mirror.

Those life-changing surgeries are performed without cost to those kids and their families.

I have seen before and after photographs of those kids' faces. It's not easy to look at the "before" images, but the "after" pictures bring a smile to my face, too.

Now, Professor, can you keep a straight face while saying those kids would be better off in a world with no religion?

So far I've only mentioned faith-based organizations. But secular humanitarian charities also depend on donors and volunteers motivated by their religious faith.

Let's look at just one small example, Camp John Marc—Special Camps for Special Kids. It is not a church camp. But it would not exist if its founders had not been motivated by religious faith, nor could the camp continue to operate without religious donors and volunteers.

As you will see in a future letter, Camp John Marc played a major role in my faith experiment and will receive some of the proceeds from this book. It is located in the Texas Hill Country just over two hours from Dallas. It is calendar beautiful. Everything is accessible by wheelchair, including two tree houses.

Each week the camp welcomes up to 140 kids who share the same kind of disability or chronic illness. They have camps for kids with cancer, muscular dystrophy, asthma, craniofacial disorders, gastrointestinal disorders, heart disease, hemophilia, HIV, juvenile arthritis, kidney disease who may on dialysis, sickle-cell anemia, spina bifida, transplants, and upper limb differences. They also have a camp for burn survivors; I'll say more about that one in a bit.

They make up great names for each week-long camp. My favorite name is the one for kids with arthritis: "The Joint Adventure."

The medical building is excellent, even though some of the kids playfully call it the "quack shack." The doctors and nurses each week are also volunteers who provide their services without cost. The campers come from families of all income levels, but none are permitted to pay.

Each child enjoys a life-changing respite from being "different." I heard one of the older campers tell some newcomers, "This is the only place I go where no one ever makes fun of me." With the benefit of special equipment for campers with disabilities, they enjoy canoeing, fishing, swimming, horseback riding, archery, arts and crafts, and camping out overnight—and they have a terrific dance (yes, kids in wheelchairs can dance).

One awesome feature of camp is a tower that resembles an old wooden oil derrick. There are several ways to the top, including some for kids who can't use their arms or legs. Once at the top, the camper's safety harness is attached to the zip line, a cable longer than a football field. It's a joy to see the thrill on the campers' faces as they speed down to the safe landing area.

When kids arrive at camp for the first time, some are crying because they've never been away from home before—except when in the hospital. By the end of the week they're crying because they don't want to leave. And they begin counting the days until they can come back next year.

Enough terrific things have happened at the camp to fill many inspiring books. I'll tell you about just one, as told to me during my first visit.

A fireman volunteered during the camp for burn survivors. One evening he and some of the campers were sitting around a campfire. Sitting beside the fireman was a ten-year-old boy whose face and body were covered with old scars from severe burns. The boy noticed the fireman's arms were also scarred, so he asked, "How'd you get burned?"

The fireman explained he went into a burning house to get a baby.

"Did you get there in time?" the camper asked.

"Yes," the fireman said, "He was a real fighter, just like you, and he pulled through."

"Where is he now?" the ten-year-old asked.

"I don't know," the fireman said.

The boy kept asking questions until they both suddenly realized where that baby was. He was now ten years old, sitting beside that fireman, asking those questions.

If you had your way, Professor, Camp John Marc would not exist.

Imagine that.

Neither would many hospitals, Catholic Relief Services, the Salvation Army, Habitat for Humanity, or Operation Smile.

Imagine that.

Neither would tens of thousands of other organizations that provide food, water, shelter, clothing, healing, and other forms of humanitarian aid to *billions* throughout the world.

Imagine that.

Babies and Bathwater

You, Professor, want to throw out the baby with the bathwater. Your aim is to get rid of all religion, not just bad religion. Lest someone think I'm exaggerating, here are your exact words: "I do everything in my power to warn people against faith itself, not just against so-called 'extremist' faith. The teachings of 'moderate' religion, though not extremist in themselves, are an open invitation to extremism."[15]

That phrase "everything in my power" makes you sound rather extremist yourself, Professor. But never mind that. Let's look at your claim that the "teachings" of religious *non*extremists "are an open invitation to extremism."

That statement, in my opinion, is the exact opposite of the truth. The most basic of all those teachings is the Golden Rule: *treat others as you would be treated in their circumstances.* In another letter I'll show that versions of the Golden Rule are found in the fundamental teachings of all major religions, and I'll discuss some practical problems regarding its application. But this much is clear: the Golden Rule is the highest point of all moral thought and the most basic commandment in every major religion. Jesus said it summed up God's Law.[16]

The Golden Rule is obviously not, as you claim, an "open invitation" to extremism. To the contrary, it forbids the kinds of extremism you complain about in your book. It's true that many who claim to be religious have committed egregious violations of the Golden Rule. But blaming religion for those violations is like blaming the crime rate on the existence of laws. If any form of religion violates the Golden Rule, it is a corrupted or counterfeit version of the original. To borrow a metaphor from Jesus, I believe that any religious rule that conflicts with the Golden Rule should be pruned from the vine.

Of course nobody's perfect. Even people who adopt the Golden Rule as their moral compass can stray off course. But there is a fundamental difference between those who encourage violations of the Golden Rule and those who endeavor to follow it religiously.

Prejudice versus Proof

You complain at length about religious terrorists and other "fanatics" and "extremists," yet you admit they won't even open a book like yours.[17] Therefore nothing you say will change them. So why do you devote so many pages to pointing out their faults? Surely your readers don't need to read a four-hundred-page book to be convinced that cruelty by religious extremists is a bad thing.

I believe I can see what you're up to. You're fanning the flames of anger toward evil religion, hoping it will spread into a prejudice against all religion. To that end, you talk about the worst religious people and never mention the best.

That tactic can be effective, but doesn't it diminish your credibility as a scientist? Painting large categories of people with the same brush has led to senseless, even deadly, hatred among families, races, and nations.

Your reason for using that tactic seems pretty obvious: you know your arguments against God don't prove your case. That's evident from several statements in your book, including your title of chapter 4: "Why There Almost Certainly Is No God." The word "almost" signals that you know your intellectual arguments fall short. So you try to make up for that shortfall by fomenting an emotional prejudice against all religion.

I've seen you use that ploy when speaking to college students. You're counting on the fact that many of them have negative feelings toward various types of religious people. They have most likely seen holy hucksters on TV who accumulate personal wealth at the expense of poor and gullible fans. And they have probably encountered sanctimonious classmates who love to confess other peoples' sins.

Pent-up resentments toward religious frauds and fanatics sometimes erupt into cheers and applause during your lectures. But those outbursts usually follow an insult aimed at noxious religious people, not a rational statement about God. Again, you never mention religious people who provide humanitarian services to *billions*.

Many atheists exaggerate some of the bad things done in the name of religion. A recurring example is the claim that the Catholic Church locked up Galileo in prison for life. In fact, that didn't happen. The church's treatment of Galileo was regrettable, and the Church eventually apologized for it. But it was not nearly as bad as atheists imply.[18] Moreover, as mentioned earlier, atheists blame religion for wars and violence that were carried out for other reasons.

However, I must admit that if all your exaggerations were deleted, some legitimate examples of religious cruelty would remain. Most of your examples involve Islamic terrorists, but some nominal Christians have also committed unconscionable acts. For proof of that, we need look no further than the official apologies issued by some major denominations. Around the turn of the millennium in 2000:

- The Roman Catholic Church issued a nineteen-thousand-word document seeking forgiveness for wrongdoings dating back centuries.
- Lutherans expressed regrets for anti-Semitic statements made by Martin Luther that led to the mistreatment of many Jews.
- Southern Baptists apologized for their complicity in racial segregation.
- Other denominations apologized for various actions of their predecessors.

I will mention one more apology that should perhaps be made.

Mutually Unfair Judgments

Some religious people judge atheists as if you were all alike. They talk as if all atheists, given enough power, would be mass murderers like Stalin, Mao, and Pol Pot. You atheists don't think that's fair. As a former part-time atheist myself, I agree with you.

However, *that is exactly how you evangelists for atheism judge people of faith.* You talk about what Thomás de Torquemada did in the Spanish Inquisition, implying that all Christians would be that cruel if they could be. But you don't mention that he was a tool of the state in Spain, or that the Pope and other church officials tried to stop him. You also condemn all religion for what nineteen ultra-fanatical Muslims did on 9/11.

In short, you seem to judge all forms of *every* religion by the worst acts of *any* religion. Yet you strongly object when people judge atheists that way. Surprisingly, Professor, *you don't deny using that double standard.* In fact, you try to justify it by saying, "Individual atheists may do evil things, but they don't do evil things in the name of atheism."[19] So if I understand you correctly, you're saying that religion motivates people to be evil, but atheism doesn't.

Please forgive me for being blunt, Professor, but I think that is one of the most outrageous claims I've ever heard—and I heard many during the forty years I practiced law.

Let's follow your reasoning through the example of Stalin, an avowed atheist whom you discuss defensively in your book. One of his goals was to eradicate religion, which Lenin had said would require the "protracted use of violence." Under Stalin, the Soviets dynamited churches and killed virtually all Orthodox priests and hundreds of thousands of Baptists.

Therefore, Professor, I was flabbergasted by your statement that there is "not the smallest evidence" that atheism influences anyone to do bad things.[20] You defend that statement by saying atheism is nothing more than the "absence of belief." Then you ask, as if rhetorically, who would do such things "for the sake of an *absence* of belief?"[21]

In the first place, I don't see how a *belief* that there is no God can be called an *absence* of belief. Nevertheless, let's assume (for the moment) you are correct and atheism just leaves a motivational vacuum. So, as you say, atheists who do evil things must be motivated "by economic greed, by political ambition, by ethnic or by racial prejudice, by deep grievance or revenge."[22] You also allow for the possibility that some atheists have been demented or insane.

Why won't you acknowledge that those factors may also account for some evil things done in the name of religion?

But never mind that. Let's get back to your position that Stalin's atheism, merely being an absence of belief, could not have *directly* motivated him to do *anything*. Are you really so naïve as to think his atheism did not at least leave him more open to murdering those millions than if he had been a devout member of the Russian Orthodox Church? If you had been one of his victims dying in a forced labor camp in Siberia, would you not have welcomed his conversion to the Christian religion?

Your claim that Stalin's atheism didn't cause him to murder those millions is like saying AIDS never killed anyone. Even if AIDS has not *directly* killed anyone, it has certainly done so indirectly. AIDS weakened their immune systems, as indicated by what AIDS stands for—acquired immune deficiency syndrome. AIDS diminished their bodies' defenses against fatal infections.

Imagine what you would have thought of a doctor in the mid-1980s if you overheard him tell a patient, "Don't worry about getting AIDS; it won't kill you," and then whisper under his breath, "At least not directly." That's no less absurd than saying atheism is harmless. Stalin's atheism left him without any religious restraints on his murderous desires.

Actually, it's worse than that. Atheism is rarely, if ever, the result of cold, intellectual reasoning devoid of anger. Atheism is often an *expression* of anger. That is obvious in books written by atheists and in testimonials on your website, Professor. Some people become atheists because they are angry with God. They want an obedient God, just as some children want obedient parents. And they vent their anger by saying God doesn't exist. Someone recently asked me, "Back when you didn't believe in God, were you an atheist or an agnostic?" I said, "When I was angry I thought of myself as an atheist; the rest of the time I suppose I was an agnostic."

Stalin may be an example of one whose atheism began as an expression of anger. His father was a drunk who beat him brutally. As a teenager Stalin enrolled in a seminary from which he was later expelled for expressing unacceptable ideas. Therefore his atheism may well have been his way of lashing out at those who had rejected him, along with everything he thought they stood for, including God.

I find it interesting, Professor, that you also became an atheist in your teens. At that age you could not have known all the things you now recite as reasons for not believing in God. So something else must have influenced you. Is it possible your own atheism is a product of unresolved anger? That would certainly explain the tone of many of your comments. But that's not for to me to decide, so let's move on to another question raised by your invitation to imagine a world with no religion.

Filling the Void

In your ideal world, Professor, everyone would be an atheist.

What would happen if you had your way? What would become of the *billions* being helped by faith-based humanitarian organizations? For that matter, what would happen to secular charities that depend on donors and volunteers motivated by their religious faith?

Would you atheists fill that void?

You have, perhaps unwittingly, admitted the answer is no, atheism cannot motivate anyone to help even one person, much less billions. Don't you recall how you tried to absolve atheism of responsibility for the atrocities committed by Stalin? You said atheism is just the "absence of belief" that can't motivate anyone to do *anything*.[23] If you're right, atheism is impotent. It can never fill the charitable void that would be left by the absence of religious faith.

Stalin's atheism certainly didn't motivate him to be charitable. Nor did it prevent him from being cruel. So how would universal atheism result in more charity and less cruelty? Your own reasoning and atheism's track record indicate just the opposite. In a world of only atheists there would be much less charity and even more cruelty.

Statistical Proof

We don't have to speculate about this. An Everest of data shows that people of faith are more charitable than secularists. They even give more to secular charities than secularists. An analysis of such data is the basis for the highly acclaimed book *Who Really Cares* by Arthur C. Brooks.[24] It is "the best study of charity that I have read" said James Q. Wilson, the preeminent scholar who advised five US presidents of both parties and received the Presidential Medal of Freedom. In the foreword to the book, Wilson called Brooks "a rigorously trained scholar" who has combined "careful studies of charity with a direct and compelling way of explaining what he has learned."[25]

Brooks found that people of faith are far more generous when it comes to:

- Donating money
- Volunteering hours
- Giving blood

Some of the data analyzed by Brooks covered a wide range of charitable activities, but he mainly talked about down-to-earth, *worldly* charity. I'm not talking about "charity" as a lawyer. That could include anything that qualifies for a charitable tax deduction, which could include donations to a tax exempt foundation promoting atheism. By "worldly" charity I mean practical help for people in need of such things as food, water, clothes, shelter, or medical treatment, those who need assistance due to disabilities, and those who need training, education, or other assistance to get out of poverty. Those are survival needs, basic quality-of-life needs. Whether something qualifies for a tax deduction is not relevant here, as that can change with politics from time to time.

I've read on your website, Professor, that you don't give to humanitarian organizations that are affiliated with religion. To be consistent, would you refuse to be treated at a Catholic hospital if you were suffering from a heart attack and were taken there in an ambulance? But I suppose you wouldn't face that dilemma if you had your way. That Catholic hospital wouldn't be there. As a result, you might not be here either.

The results would be catastrophic if everyone adhered to your policy against giving to religious charities. The data analyzed by Brooks shows that many *secular* charities would also go out of business, as they depend on religious supporters. And the more religious people are, the more generous they tend to be. Those who attend worship services once a week give three and a half times more than those who only go once or twice a year. But the latter give more than secularists *even if you don't count their contributions to churches and other religious institutions.*

Some publicity about the book *Who Really Cares* spotlighted the finding that political conservatives give more to charity than liberals, but that was an indirect and secondary correlation. The book makes it clear that liberals who are religious give almost as much as conservatives who are religious. Religion trumps politics when it comes to charity.[26]

Some atheists say Europeans are more enlightened than Americans because they are less religious. However, Brooks points out that Americans voluntarily give more to charity than every country in Europe, whether measured per capita, in absolute dollars, or as a percentage of gross national product.

Without even mentioning the findings made by Brooks, you claim that when it comes to making moral decisions, "there is no statistically significant difference between atheists and believers."[27] You base that claim on the book *Moral Minds* by Marc Hauser. But Hauser's book does not support your claim. At most, it supports the idea that both atheists and believers have an "innate sense" of what they *should* do. That's not the issue. Even the Bible says God's Law, as summed up by the Golden Rule, is written in all human hearts.[28]

The book by Hauser was based on responses to hypothetical questions posed over the Internet. For example, people were asked what they would do if they saw a child drowning in a shallow pond and no one else was there to help, but it would ruin their trousers if they saved the child. Of course almost everybody said they would save the child. The other questions were also about hypothetical emergencies not likely to happen in real life, such as having to make an instant choice between saving one person's life or saving several others. Again, both religious and nonreligious people gave similar answers. But they were sitting at computers answering questions about hypothetical moral dilemmas they never really expected to face.

Hauser's book is 426 pages long, but it contains no serious analysis of the moral disparity between believers and atheists when it comes to actual *behaviors*. The issue here is not whether people instinctively *know* the Golden Rule, but whether and to what extent they actually comply with it. Arthur Brooks (author of *Who Really Cares*, referred to previously) found that religious people abide by the Golden Rule far more than anyone else. They not only commit more major acts of charity, they perform more routine acts of kindness. People of faith are more likely to give up their seats to older people on crowded buses, give food or money to a homeless person, and return excess change mistakenly given to them by cashiers.

Brooks based his finding on huge volumes of data about what people *do*, and concluded:

> [T]he evidence leaves no room for doubt. Religious people are far more charitable than nonreligious people. In years of research, I have never found a measurable way in which secularists are more charitable than religious people.[29]

Of course not all religious people are charitable and not all charitable people are religious. I know people who are not outwardly religious but regularly volunteer for humanitarian organizations. But again, those organizations would not exist if religious people did not support them. The fact remains that most worldly charity can be traced to religious faith.

Research also shows that being religious, giving to charity, and volunteering is good for us—and not being religious is bad for us.[30] Dr. Frank I. Luntz reports on studies showing that people who say they are not at all religious are at "the very bottom of the happiness index," and the angriest people are atheists and agnostics.[31]

Withholding Relevant Evidence

Most books by atheists never mention major positive contributions of the Christian religion. We lawyers call that "withholding evidence." (I'm talking about Christianity because it is the largest religion and is the one I chose to follow for reasons I'll explain in a separate letter.)

History shows that Christians have been responsible for:

- Introducing charity on a larger scale than the world had ever seen
- Starting public hospitals
- Establishing universities
- Fostering individual freedom
- Opposing slavery
- Promoting the rule of law
- Advancing science (contrary to a common misperception)

An excellent account of these world-changing contributions can be found in *Christianity on Trial* by Vincent Carroll and David Shiflett.[32] The authors were not religious professionals and their research was impeccable. Their book was published several years before yours,

Professor, but you don't mention it. Isn't that a serious omission for someone who claims to be an objective scientist?

One way professional atheists withhold evidence is to tell only one side of the story. For example, Christopher Hitchens accused the Dutch Reform Church of helping to maintain apartheid in South Africa, but he neglected to mention the role of the Anglican Church in ending it.

Another example concerns the history of slavery in your country, Professor. Atheists point out that some rich Christians in England were slave traders. But they fail to mention that the fight against slavery was led by a Christian evangelist in your parliament, William Wilberforce. His mentor was John Newton, who became a clergyman after repenting from his career as the captain of a slave ship. Newton is mainly remembered for writing the most loved hymn in history, "Amazing Grace." Appropriately, that is also the name of a movie recounting the efforts of Wilberforce to abolish slavery.

Christians are still freeing slaves. During one five-year period, Christian Solidarity International freed over twenty-one thousand slaves in Sudan.[33] And they have continued to free slaves there and elsewhere. Their methods are both peaceful and legal; they buy the slaves and grant them freedom. Then they provide them with food, clothing, shelter, and medical help. When possible, they reunite them with their families.

This isn't theory. This is reality. Those former slaves are living in freedom thanks to committed Christians.

Listen to Yourself

Imagine you are about to speak to an audience of those former slaves. Before being rescued by Christian Solidarity International they had been abused in almost every way imaginable. Now they and their families are free, well fed, and safe.

Take a deep breath and imagine the gratitude coursing through their veins.

Now pretend that you begin your speech by telling them you are an atheist and then continue with the following remarks:

> Despite everything Christians have done for you—and for billions more around the world—there have been other Christians who were not so kind. Some were downright cruel, especially five hundred years ago during the Spanish Inquisition. That is why I have made it my mission in life to rid the world of religion—*all* religion. I see the puzzled expressions on your faces. You're wondering why I would want to get rid of good religion along with the bad. Well, I'll tell you why. We can't be too careful. There is always a risk that some good religious groups will be taken over by bad people. It's happened before and could happen again. So I want to eliminate all religion, no exceptions.
>
> But fear not. After all religion has been ex-terminated, we atheists will make the personal and financial sacrifices needed to help the down-

trodden, disabled, and otherwise disadvantaged, just as Christians are doing for you today. And I promise we won't turn bad like Stalin, Mao, and Pol Pot. How can you be sure of that despite the terrible track records of nations ruled by atheists? Why should you believe atheists will start doing all the humanitarian work now being done by Christians? You will just have to trust me. So join me in the fight to rid the planet of religious faith. Begin right now by letting go of your own faith. Become an atheist! You don't have to be certain there is no God. Atheism is really just a choice.

Face it, Professor. If you gave a speech like that the audience would wonder if you were being satirical or if you were out of your mind. Yet I believe that imaginary speech is a fair summary of what you and other professional atheists are trying to sell us in your books.

The next time a natural disaster strikes, go talk to people being helped by the Salvation Army. Try to convince them they would be better off if there were no religion. Tell them you atheists will help them after the Salvation Army is gone. But you'd better be prepared to explain why you are not *already* organized to help in emergencies like that.

Then go talk to a family for whom Habitat for Humanity is building a house. Tell them they would be better off if those Habitat people would get over their God delusion.

Sorry, Professor, but as philosophers here in Texas say, "That dog won't hunt."

A False Assumption

Atheists talk as if religion were one monolithic organism. You assume those nineteen terrorists who brought us 9/11 demonstrated an evil gene, not only in their version of Islam, but in all religions. Yet it makes no sense to blame all of Christianity, Judaism, Hinduism, and Buddhism for such madness. It's not even fair to Islam, as those terrorists violated prohibitions in the Quran.[34] Moreover, one study found that "the majority of young [Muslim] men who joined terrorist groups grew up in secular homes and knew very little about Islam."[35]

I spent a lot of time on business in an Islamic country over a twenty-year period. I knew Muslims who were just as repulsed by the actions of Islamic terrorists as anyone. They were also embarrassed because they knew many people would judge them by the actions of those terrorists. That is exactly what professional atheists (and some Christians) do when they talk as if all Muslims were in league with terrorists.

The 9/11 attacks spawned numerous books on terrorism. Speaking about one of those books—*What Terrorists Want* by Louise Richardson—Harvard professor Stanley Hoffmann said, "If a reader has the time to read only one book on terrorism, this is that book." Richardson points out that in 1968 there were eleven known terrorist groups, *none* of which had any kind of religious affiliation. By the mid-1990s there were fifty known groups, only about a dozen of which had religious motivations.[36]

Therefore, Professor, your assumption that all terrorist groups are religious is simply wrong. In fact, many terrorists have been atheists.[37]

There are billions of religious people in the world. They follow many different religions that are further divided into countless subgroups. Christianity is divided into an estimated thirty-seven thousand competing denominations.[38] Christians are all over the map, geographically, theologically, and liturgically. Yet you quote a few controversial figures as if they spoke for all Christians—but you're quick to point out that neither Joseph Stalin nor Madalyn Murray O'Hair spoke for all atheists.

Christian "fundamentalists" have been criticized a lot, not only by atheists but by other Christians. But not all fundamentalists are alike, either. One of them told me, "I am a fundamentalist, not a judgmentalist. I accept the Bible as infallible, but *I'm* not infallible. So I don't judge anyone for disagreeing with me, not even about the Bible." He assured me there are many more like him, but they neither seek nor receive much attention. That's because they don't spend a lot of time arguing about how the Bible came to be written. They think it's more important to spend that time doing what the Bible tells them to do, especially for the poor and hungry.

Everyone knows that some members of the clergy have been an embarrassment to others. That's true of every professional grouping, most certainly including mine and yours—lawyers and professors. And the embarrassing ones attract more attention. But I've spent time in places where there is no Christian clergy. I have always returned home with a deeper appreciation for their influence in my country and community. I've also spent a lot of time in your country, Professor. All things considered, I think we both should say, "Thank God for the Christian clergy."

Of course religion is no exception to the rule that great causes attract some fanatics, fools, and frauds. But that doesn't make them bad causes. Consider the environmental movement for example. It has spawned the word "ecoterrorism" and newspaper stories like this: "Four environmental extremists pleaded guilty to arson and conspiracy . . . for their part in a five-year wave of fire bombings."[39] While practicing law in Alaska I had to deal with some environmental extremists who were clearly irrational. But that's no reason to throw the entire environmental movement overboard. It deserves some credit for improvements in the air we breathe, in the water we drink, and in the food we eat.

All human institutions—governmental, scientific, educational, environmental, charitable, and religious—have been used for bad purposes. But getting rid of them would plunge the world even deeper into chaos and misery.

Ignoring Mount Everest

In the preface to the paperback edition of *The God Delusion* you finally respond to those who have been saying, "You always attack the worst of religion and ignore the best." *And, at last, you acknowledge there is a good kind of religion.* In fact, you go so far as to say, "If only such subtle, nuanced religion predominated, the world would surely be a better place, and I would have written a different book. The melancholy truth is that this kind of understated, decent, revisionist religion is numerically negligible."[40]

So your excuse for not having mentioned good religion is that it is "numerically negligible." But you don't cite one scintilla of data to support that statement. Nor do you really explain what you're talking about. The adjectives you use to describe the religion that would make the world a "better place"—subtle, nuanced, understated, decent, revisionist—are not exactly, well, exact. The only other clue you give is to call it the religion of "sophisticated theologians" like Paul Tillich and Dietrich Bonhoeffer.[41] My friends who are religious scholars tell me that Tillich and Bonhoeffer certainly made significant contributions to the field of theology, but it's ludicrous to say their "sophisticated" writings represent the only good kind of religion.

Once again, Professor, you maintain a stubborn silence about religious people who provide humanitarian help to *billions* every year. Your claim that they are "numerically negligible" is crushed by the Everest of data referred to earlier in this letter. You even remain silent about them in your rebuttal to those who accuse you of attacking the worst of religion and ignoring the best.

Your silence proves their point.

Making Matters Worse

You say getting rid of good religion would be a price worth paying to get rid of evil religion. *Even if that were true, which it isn't, that is not what you are doing.* You admit religious extremists won't even open a book like yours.[42] So you are not making a dent in the kind of religion you complain about. On the other

> You admit religious extremists won't even open a book like yours.

hand, you have persuaded some nonextremists to give up their religion.[43]

The net result is that you have reduced the pool of religious folks most likely to practice charity. But you have not reduced the number of extremists who violate the Golden Rule with impunity.

That's throwing out the baby *instead* of the bathwater.

Even though you are an atheist, Professor, you are also a scientist, or at least a science teacher. Can't you be objective enough to see the good being done by religion? One of the best books I've read showing the benefits of religion was written by an atheist. I mentioned it earlier: *An Atheist Defends Religion* by Bruce Sheiman. In his introduction he says his book "will persuasively show that atheism is an impoverished belief system, and that individually and collectively, we are much better off with religion that without it." He goes on to say, "Religion's misdeeds may make for provocative history, but the everyday good works of billions of people is the real history of religion, one that parallels the growth and prosperity of humankind."[44] In a section headed "Empirical Evidence Atheists Cannot Deny," Sheiman shows that religion is associated with every aspect of a fulfilled life—altruism and generosity, meaning and purpose, coping skills, social connections and fellowship, optimism and hope, gratitude and forgiveness, martial satisfaction and family commitment, and healthy lifestyle choices.[45]

Sheiman candidly admits, "I sincerely want to believe in a personal God, in the soul and the afterlife."[46] I once felt the same way—and in another letter I'll explain how I finally did come to believe in those things.

However, the fact that an atheist can see the benefits of religion does lead to an interesting question: Are good things done by religious people really evidence of God?

Religion versus God

The comedian Woody Allen said, "If I'm sitting next to a guy and he has true belief, I look at him and think, *Poor thing, you really are deluded.* But his life is much better than mine."[47]

I've heard you argue, Professor, that even if religion is good for us and atheism is bad for us, that doesn't prove there is a God.

You're forgetting something. *You* are the one who treats religious behaviors as relevant to the God issue. *You* are the one who treats bad religion as evidence against God, but refuse to treat good religion as evidence of God.

Make up your mind. You can't have it both ways. Either religious behavior is relevant to the God issue, or it isn't. If it isn't, why do you spend so much time talking about it? If it is, why do you ignore all the good it does?

In any event, I have done what you asked. I have imagined a world with no religion. Frankly, Professor, I don't believe you would want to live in that world yourself. As a matter of fact, you might not be *able* to live in it if you needed one of the hospitals that would be missing.

That said, however, I acknowledge that it's possible to believe religion is a force for good and still have doubts about God. Therefore, in my next letter, I will continue this discussion by narrowing the focus to the question: Does God exist?

Sincerely,

John

Letter No. 2

Regarding God

Dear Professor:
The first book I read defending atheism was *Why I Am Not a Christian* by Bertrand Russell. That was over fifty years ago when I was a student at Baylor University. Thanks to a course in logic, I could see his arguments were not conclusive. But that logic course had been a double-edged sword. It led me to think that some of my religious beliefs were nonsense. I finally overreacted and threw out my belief in God with the nonsense. That void was soon filled with far more disturbing doubts about atheism. So I kept looking for arguments on both sides.

I eventually noticed that atheists don't claim to be sure they're right. Even Bertrand Russell knew he couldn't prove there is no God.[48] And I appreciate you, Professor, for being honest enough to acknowledge your atheism is an "assumption" that you "cannot know for certain" is correct.[49] Some atheists make that concession reluctantly, as if confessing a crime. But you are straightforward about it. You include the word "almost" in what you call your

> Therefore, atheism is a
> decision, not a discovery.
> It is a choice. It is choosing
> to guess there is no God.
> No matter how confident
> anyone claims to feel about
> that guess, it is still a guess.

main conclusion: "God almost certainly does not exist."[50] I saw an interview in which you were asked if that leaves open the possibility that God *does* exist. Without hesitation you said, "Any scientist would leave open that possibility . . . We can't be dogmatic and say it is certain that God doesn't exist."[51]

Therefore, atheism is a decision, not a discovery. It is a choice. It is choosing to guess there is no God. No matter how confident anyone claims to feel about that guess, it is still a guess.

God and Unicorns

You and other atheists try to downplay the fact that you can't prove your case. You use variations of an old line about unicorns or some other mythical figure, such as: I can't prove God doesn't exist, but neither can I prove unicorns don't exist.[52] Of course you're implying there's no more reason to explore the possibility that God exists than the possibility that unicorns are real.

Let me ask you:

- How many people have been inspired by their belief in unicorns to start organizations like the Salvation Army, Catholic Relief Services, Habitat for Humanity, and thousands of other organizations that help billions in need of food, water, clothes, shelter, and other kinds of humanitarian assistance?

- How many people have felt led by their belief in unicorns to establish hospitals and other medical institutions like those built by Anglicans, Baptists, Catholics, Jews, Lutherans, Methodists, Mormons, and Presbyterians?
- How many universities have been founded by people who believed in unicorns, as compared to those founded by people of faith, like Notre Dame, Princeton, and thousands more?
- How many people who believe in unicorns have been awarded Nobel Prizes in science, medicine, and peace?
- How many scholars once thought unicorns didn't exist but changed their minds and wrote books to persuade others to believe in unicorns?
- How many alcoholics and addicts have remained clean and sober through a program that involves placing faith in a "higher unicorn"?
- How many convicted felons have become law-abiding citizens through prison programs based on faith in unicorns?
- How many lives have been saved by humanitarian organizations that depend on volunteers and donors motivated by their faith in unicorns?
- How many people would die if everyone who believed in unicorns stopped giving blood?
- How many have been saved from thoughts of suicide by praying to unicorns?

- How many have found purpose and meaning in their lives by placing faith in unicorns?
- How many find comfort and peace in times of grief by praying to unicorns?
- Does placing faith in unicorns create hope for eternal joy?
- Does *not* placing faith in unicorns involve a risk of eternal regrets?
- Can you test the idea that unicorns exist by living as if they do?
- Is there *any* compelling reason to explore the possibility that unicorns exist?

When these same questions are asked about believing in God, the answers are dramatically different. You can't dodge the significance of those answers by saying they don't prove God exists. They're not intended to prove God exists. But they do show why the mere *possibility* of God's existence is not a frivolous matter to be tossed aside with a flippant comment about unicorns, Zeus, or Mother Goose.

So let's take an honest look at what's behind your decision to guess there is no God. Since your field is science, I'll begin with a short discussion on whether science sheds any light on the issue.

God and Science

I was shocked, Professor, that your four-hundred-page book doesn't mention Professor Antony Flew except in one footnote.[53] For decades he was the intellectual champion for atheism. Then he changed his mind and accepted the existence of God. Moreover, your footnote doesn't discuss Flew's scientific reasons for changing his mind, which he called "compelling and irrefutable."[54] Your fellow atheists Christopher Hitchens, Sam Harris, and Daniel Dennett don't mention Professor Flew at all in their best sellers, not even in footnotes. That's like writing a book on the history of science and failing to mention Albert Einstein.

Your lone footnote mentioning Flew attempts to dismiss him by referring to his "old age." You should have done a little math before saying that. Get ready to blush as I explain why: When you wrote that footnote you were several years older than Flew was when he began to change his mind. You apparently based your reference to Flew's age (eighty-one) on the date he made headlines by mentioning his belief in God in 2004 at New York University. But that wasn't the very day he changed his mind. It wasn't even the same decade. Flew had begun to reconsider and reject atheism over twenty years before that, in the early 1980s. As he said in his book, "I confessed at that point that atheists have to be embarrassed by . . . scientific proof . . . that the universe had a beginning."[55]

At that point Flew was only in his late *fifties*. You, Professor, were in your middle *sixties* when you made that snide comment about his "old age." Were you trying to avoid looking at the real "Flew" in your atheistic soup—his scientific *reasons* for believing in God?

Your reference to Flew's age reminds me of how some people try to discredit others by referring to their race or gender. The older I get, the more I agree with Norman Vincent Peale, who said, "Ageism is as odious as racism and sexism." So I feel your reference to Flew's "old age" would have been offensive even if you had not been factually mistaken.

Not being a scientist, I will not pretend to understand all the scientific data that convinced Flew that God exists. On the other hand, I don't want to leave the impression that I don't know anything about science. Early in my legal career I had to cross-examine an opponent's expert witness who not only was as smart as a rocket scientist, he really *was* a rocket scientist—with NASA. To prepare for that I gave myself a crash course in certain areas of science. In the years that followed I represented clients in legal proceedings involving scientific evidence. I wrote countless contracts for geophysicists, geologists, and engineers in the petroleum industry. My practical understanding of what they did was enhanced by the fact that I had worked summers in the Texas oil fields while in high school, college, and law school. And my knowledge of science has been expanded by reading books like Stephen Hawkins's *A Brief History of Time: From the Big Bang to Black Holes.*

I'm still no expert in any major field of science. But it isn't necessary to be an expert to spot a serious flaw that permeates your book: the assumption that no competent scientist can believe in God.

With all due respect, Professor, your credentials pale in comparison to those of many scientists who do believe in God. They include Nobel laureates such as Arthur Compton, Arno Penzias, Max Born, William D.

With all due respect, Professor, your credentials pale in comparison to those of many scientists who do believe in God.

Phillips, and Charles Townes (all in physics) and Ernst Boris Chain (physiology and medicine). Dr. Townes also received the Templeton Prize for contributions in the understanding of religion.

Other scientists with résumés equal or superior to yours have written books about their personal faith, including Michael Guillen, Francis S. Collins, John Polkinghorne, Russell Stannard, and Timothy Johnson, just to name a few.[56]

Many world-class scientists were named in a 1998 *Newsweek* cover story, "Science Finds God."[57] Thousands of scientists are members of the American Scientific Affiliation: A Fellowship of Christians in Science.[58]

Your assumption that no competent scientist can believe in God is belied by your own book, Professor. You made an admiring reference to Jocelyn Bell Burnell, the scientist who discovered pulsars.[59] Apparently you didn't know she is a Christian. You can read her personal testimony, along with those of other scientists, in *Spiritual Evolution*.[60]

A famous survey done in 1916—and repeated in the late 1990s—asked a thousand scientists if they believed in God. The survey was slanted (perhaps unintentionally) to elicit a negative response. It didn't just ask if they believed in God. It asked if they believed in "a God in intellectual and affective communication with humankind" and to whom people can pray "in expectation of receiving an answer." I might have answered no to that myself, as I don't believe God always gives direct and affirmative answers to prayers. Like many other believers, I'm thankful I *don't* always get what I pray for. Notwithstanding that loaded question in the survey, about 42 percent said they believed in that kind of God. About the same percent said they didn't, and the rest either said they weren't sure or didn't answer.[61]

A more recent survey by the Pew Forum on Religion & Public Life found that "just over half of scientists (51 percent) believe in some form of deity or higher power."[62] (The other 49 percent was a mix of those who said they didn't believe, weren't sure, or didn't respond to the survey.)

It's true that the percentage of scientists who believe in God is not as high as that of the general public. But many of them had parents who were nonbelievers. It's no surprise that students from that background would be more interested in the natural sciences. But their unbelief *preceded* their scientific education; it did not result from it.

In any event, counting scientists who believe in God doesn't resolve the issue. God's existence obviously doesn't depend on their votes.

Evolution

As a zoologist you have written a lot about evolution, and you talk as if a belief in evolution makes it hard to believe in God. Some religious people agree with you on that point. I respectfully disagree.

I realize there are competing theories of evolution, but there's no reason to go into all those here except to note that even you evolutionists disagree over what has and has not been proven. I don't claim to know beyond the last tiny speck of doubt whether any of the various theories of evolution is correct. But if I were absolutely certain that at least one of them is correct, and that it applies to the human species, my faith would not be affected.

In his book *Thank God for Evolution*, the Christian minister Michael Dowd says the theory of evolution supports the view that we are the result of divine design, not blind chance.[63] I won't comment on the merits of his opinion but it does show that a belief in evolution does not preclude a belief in God. And his book has been praised by six Nobel laureates.

Dr. Francis S. Collins has been called "one of world's most distinguished scientists" by William D. Phillips, 1997 Nobel laureate in physics. Dr. Collins was head of the Human Genome Project, which achieved one of the greatest scientific breakthroughs in history: mapping the human DNA. Dr. Collins is a Christian who has written a book in which he tells about his journey from atheism to faith—*The Language of God*. While it's not the main point of his book, he explains why he believes in both God *and* evolution.[64]

I know Christians who call themselves "creationists" but still believe in evolution. They cite a passage in the Bible indicating that what seems like a very long time to us is almost nothing to God.[65] They say God created everything, no matter how long it took according to the way we mortals reckon time. Their view does seem consistent with what Einstein said about relativity.

On the other hand, there are many sincerely religious people who are troubled by the theory of evolution. I annoyed one of them by mentioning the title of the book *Did Adam and Eve Have Navels?* He took that to be a serious question and emphatically said the answer is no. He explained that Adam and Eve were created, not born, so they had no umbilical cords, hence no navels. He obviously rejected the theory of evolution. But the fact remains that no one has to reject it to believe in God. One doesn't even have to form an opinion about it.

The atheist Sam Harris mentions one particular argument against evolution as if it were a majority view held among believers. The argument says the universe is just over six thousand years old, which doesn't leave enough time for evolution. That view is based on a theory that the earth was created on October 23, 4004 BC, a date calculated by Archbishop Ussher in 1650 based on his interpretations of some Old Testament genealogies. Sam Harris says 53 percent of Americans accept that view.[66] Harris is simply wrong. I'm surprised the real number is as high as it is—18 percent.[67] But Harris grossly exaggerates that figure in an apparent effort to belittle more people who believe in God.

Scientific Mistakes by Religious People

Atheists like to say the history of religion is littered with scientific mistakes. But that is even truer of the history of science. In my first letter I mentioned the book *When Science Goes Wrong*. The first paragraph points out that "for every brilliant scientific success there are a dozen failures."[68] Even Galileo and Einstein made mistakes. Experts in every field of study make mistakes *every day* according to David Freedman, author of *Wrong: Why Experts Keep Failing Us*. He explains how experts, including "scientists, finance wizards, doctors, relationship gurus, celebrity CEOs, high-powered consultants, health officials, and more," are constantly misleading us.[69] But it would be absurd to do away with all those professions—with the possible exception of "finance wizards." (Just kidding.)

To summarize: nobody has to deny any scientifically proven fact to believe in God. Some highly respected scientists believe there is enough evidence to prove there is a God. But like most folks, I don't know enough science to fully understand all their arguments. So let's move on to another approach, one that scientists and nonscientists alike have followed to an unshakable belief in God.

Just Three Options

When it comes to a belief in God, people generally agree that there are three options—to be an atheist, an agnostic, or a person of faith. But some argue about the definitions of those terms. For example, some say an atheist who has any doubt is really an agnostic. But you, Professor, say you'd be surprised to find an atheist who claims to be certain he's right.[70] Conversely, some say a believer who ever has a moment of doubt is really an agnostic—but most believers would disagree with that.

So I want to be clear about what I mean by "atheist," "agnostic," and "person of faith."

Definitions

My definitions will follow your lead, Professor. You describe yourself as one who says, "I cannot know for certain but I think God is very improbable, and I live my life on the assumption that he is not there."[71] I like that as a definition. You use the word "assumption," but your operative phrase is, "live my life." So your definition is not limited to idle thoughts—it is about how you choose to live.

Using your model, I will use these definitions:

- **Person of faith:** one who chooses to live his or her life on the assumption that God exists
- **Atheist:** one who chooses to live his or her life on the assumption that God does *not* exist
- **Agnostic:** one who does not choose to live his or her life based on either assumption.

Some religious people don't like to see the word "assumption" in a definition of faith because it leaves room for some uncertainty. But a person who is 100 percent certain needs no "faith." Some say acting on faith can lead to certainty based on experience. I've come to agree with them, but I'll discuss that in another letter. Right now I will focus on the threshold question: What are the options of one who is not absolutely certain that God does or does not exist?

Options

You've acknowledged that atheism can't be proved. Let us assume for the moment that God's existence can't be proved either, at least not by one person to another. That leaves three options:

- **Option 1:** be a person of faith by choosing to assume God exists.
- **Option 2:** be an atheist by choosing to assume God doesn't exist.

- **Option 3:** be an agnostic by not choosing to make either assumption.

The first two are choices. The third can be a choice or the result of not making a choice.

Those who wait on absolutely certainty may never make a choice. Of course that's not exactly a profound observation. That's true of every option we face—regarding our education, jobs, marriages, children, places to live, medical treatments, where and what we eat, how we invest, and what to do for recreation. Driving a car involves many life-or-death choices that must be made without certain knowledge of all the relevant facts. As Thomas Edison said, "We don't know a millionth of 1 percent about anything." Therefore, every option we choose could be called an act of faith.

When it comes to the options regarding God, Albert Camus, a Nobel laureate in literature, said, "I would rather live my life as if there is a God and die to find out there isn't, than live my life as if there isn't and die to find out there is." Of course that statement assumes the possibility of an afterlife. But to be a person of faith would be the best way to live even if you assume this is the only life there is. My first letter explains why that is true, and the mere possibility of an afterlife makes the option of faith even more

Albert Camus, a Nobel laureate in literature, said, "I would rather live my life as if there is a God and die to find out there isn't, than live my life as if there isn't and die to find out there is."

compelling—and no one can rule out that possibility. The atheist Sam Harris stated the obvious when he said, "We do not know what awaits each of us after death, but we know we will die."[72] After the famous atheist Christopher Hitchens was diagnosed with cancer I saw him in a TV interview. When asked if he objected to the fact that people were praying for him, he seemed to hedge his bet by saying, "They have my blessing."

Here are some possible outcomes of the three options:

- If people of faith have made the right choice, they have a chance of being glad they did. If they have made a wrong choice, they will never know it.
- If atheists have made a wrong choice, they may live to regret it. If they have made the right choice, they will never know it.
- Agnostics are the only ones who can be sure they have *not* made the right choice—because they haven't made one. They will either never know the difference or regret not having chosen the first option.

Choosing "Right Regrets"

The writer Arthur Miller said, "Maybe all one can do is hope to end up with the right regrets." That's a bit too pessimistic for me, but it's close to some advice I often gave while practicing law. When a client was having a hard time choosing between two or more options—all of which could have unwanted consequences—I suggested, "Pretend that no matter which one you choose, you're going to regret it. Which choice would you regret the least?"

It's amazing how often that proved to be a break-through. For example, in a bad real estate market for sellers, one client received a take-it-or-leave-it offer for a property he really needed to sell. He was agonizing over the possibility that he might get a little higher price from someone else if he rejected the offer. So I said, "If you don't accept it you might have to sell it for less or not be able to sell it at all. Will you regret that more than taking the offer and finding out later you could have gotten a little more?"

He quickly accepted the offer and never looked back.

I often make decisions that way myself. It has led me to make some conservative choices and some that were courageous, depending on what was at stake. I have passed up many get-rich-quick "opportunities" because I didn't like the downside risks.

I finally asked myself that kind of question about God: *If I'm going to live as if God exists or live as if God does not exist, which would I rather regret if it turns out to be wrong?*

My students call that a no-brainer.

As you know, Professor, this line of thinking is sometimes called "Pascal's Wager." For readers not familiar with that term, it refers to an essay found among the papers of Blaise Pascal after his death in the 1600s. He had been a brilliant young scientist, mathematician, and inventor, who became known as the father of the theory of probability. In his "Wager" essay he com-

I finally asked myself that kind of question about God: If I'm going to live as if God exists or live as if God does not exist, which would I rather regret if it turns out to be wrong?

pared faith in God to placing a bet and said, "If you win, you win everything; if you lose, you lose nothing."[73]

Although Pascal is given credit for that thought, a Muslim philosopher had written it many years earlier.[74] In fact, it's so obvious that many who have never heard of Pascal regard it as common sense. I once worked in the oil fields with an older gentleman who was known for being wise, kind, and religious. One day another worker asked him, "What makes you think there's a God?" He shrugged and said, "Why take a chance?"

Avoiding the Obvious

I've read scores of attempts to refute Pascal's Wager, including yours, Professor.[75] They all remind me of the following story that gave me a smile.

Still swaggering from his recent promotion to the rank of captain, an arrogant military officer was speaking to his troops.

A private ran up to him with a message from headquarters.

The captain assumed it was another letter of congratulations, so he told the private to read it out loud.

"But sir," the private whispered, "It's marked PERSONAL."

"I gave you an order, son," the captain said. "Read it."

So the private read it, loud enough for all to hear. It said: "Captain, you are proving to be the most incompetent officer I have ever seen. If you do not shape up within a week's time I shall remove you from command and reduce you in rank."

Signed: "Colonel Smith."

Immediately the captain said, "Good job, private. Now go and have that message decoded."

Every attempt I've seen to refute Pascal's Wager has been like that—a futile attempt to avoid the obvious. One common criticism still surprises me every time I see it. It rejects Pascal's point because he didn't spell out specific instructions on *how* to live as if God exists. That's like telling a doctor, "You have said I have cancer and may die from it if I don't undergo treatment. But you haven't specified what treatment I should get. And there are many different options, including chemotherapy, radiation, special diets, and various types of surgery. And you can't guarantee any of them will work. Therefore I reject your diagnosis, and I shall assume I don't have cancer and my life is not at risk."

Of course any such patient would be in denial and overlooking the possibility that more than one treatment could work—and choosing any of them might be safer than rejecting them all.

Actually, Pascal's essay was not silent about how to live as if God exists, but he wasn't very specific. So I will offer some suggestions for that in my next letter. But right now I want to stay focused on his diagnosis of the underlying risk.

Five False Assumptions about Pascal's Wager

False Assumption No. 1:

Pascal's Wager was intended to prove God exists.

Pascal did not claim that particular essay proved there is a God. To the contrary, he began the essay by saying we are *incapable* of knowing if God exists.[76] Pascal eventually did become confident of God's existence, but not for any reason given in that essay. Its purpose was to answer the question: Assuming we *can't* be certain there is a God, should we live as if there is a God or live as if there isn't?

False Assumption No. 2:

Pascal's Wager is only useful for someone who regards God's existence as a close question.

In the documentary movie *Expelled* Ben Stein asked you, Professor, to place a percentage on your level of confidence that there is no God. You said, "I'm not comfortable putting a figure on it."[77]

In your book *The God Delusion* you describe a continuum of confidence with seven "milestones."[78] Milestone No. 1 is absolute certainty that God exists. The opposite extreme is No. 7, absolute certainty that God does not exist. You say you'd be surprised find anyone at No. 7, but you included it for "symmetry." Then you place yourself at No. 6, saying you feel God's existence is "very improbable."

Since you guess the probability of God is low, you feel Pascal's Wager doesn't come into play. You would have a different view if you placed the odds on God closer to Milestone No. 4 on your scale, "Exactly 50 percent."

That presents three problems. First, you acknowledge your seven-point scale is an exercise in "human judgments."[79] In other words, it's guesswork. Second, your guesswork won't change reality. No one can guess God into or out of existence. Third, you don't give any weight to the different consequences of being wrong. I'll bet you don't make other important decisions that way. I suspect, for example, you would never play Russian roulette with a six-shooter, not even for a large reward, even though the odds would be five-to-one in your favor. Likewise, anything short of absolute certainty that God does *not* exist—*which you acknowledge is not attainable*—makes betting against God a reckless thing to do.

False Assumption No. 3:
Pascal's Wager makes sense only if you believe in an afterlife.

This is wrong for two reasons. First, as discussed in my previous letter, living as if God exists is the best way to live even if we could be certain there will be no life beyond this one. Second, the wisdom of Pascal's Wager does not depend on a *belief* in an afterlife. It is the wisest choice because we can't rule out the *possibility* of an afterlife. As mentioned earlier, even the avowed atheist Sam Harris acknowledges we can't be sure of what awaits us after death. And many people sense the truth in something said by the Jesuit scientist Pierre Teilhard de Chardin: "We are not human beings having a spiritual experience; we are spiritual beings having a human experience."

Benjamin Franklin said, "The soul of man is immortal and will be treated with justice in another life respecting its conduct in this one." Unless we can completely rule out *any possibility* that he was right, it makes good sense to be a person of faith. And most of us are imbued with the feeling that he was right; justice will eventually be done.

Of course the possibility of ultimate justice involves the concept of fairness. Some people say there's no such thing as a natural standard of fairness. But if you spend enough time with them you will likely hear them say, "That's not fair." You, Professor, have said you dislike "unfairness."[80] That makes no sense if there were no such thing as fairness. Your fellow atheist Christopher Hitchens acknowledged there is an "innate sense of fairness."[81]

We may disagree over how the law of fairness applies in specific situations, but we all sense there should be consequences for those who violate it. And we can't rule out the possibility that there will be another life in which we will be held accountable for how we lived in this one. Pascal's point was that betting against that possibility is unwise.

Either God exists or God does not exist. If God does exist, either we will be held accountable for how we lived this life, or we won't. If it's a mistake to live as if there will be such an accounting, that's a mistake we can afford to make. That's not true of the other options. The better-safe-than-sorry choice is clear.

False Assumption No. 4:
To make Pascal's "wager," all one must do is believe God exists.

You, Professor, assume Pascal said it's enough to give intellectual assent to the proposition that God exists. Then you say God would surely require more, such as "kindness, or generosity, or humility."[82] But if you will read the rest of Pascal's essay you will see he would *agree* with you on that point. He said if you bet on God, "You will be faithful, honest, humble, grateful, doing good, a sincere and true friend."[83]

So Pascal never said it's enough to assume God exists. It must be an *operating* assumption. It must be a *working* hypothesis. An idle guess is not sufficient. As discussed earlier, a person of faith is one who chooses "to live his or her life" based on the assumption that God exists. That is an active commitment, not a passive assumption. Your assumption that Pascal was only talking about the latter is simply not correct.

False Assumption No. 5:
Pascal recommended a fraudulent faith.

You accuse Pascal of urging people to feign or force a belief in God.[84] Then you point out that God surely can't be fooled by a false faith. But as one who studies science, Professor, you know perfectly well that we don't have to force ourselves to believe a hypothesis before putting it to the test of acting as if it's true. It's not unusual for a scientist to prove something is true when he didn't expect that result.

Avoidance

I once thought defenders of atheism were deliberately misrepresenting Pascal's Wager. I may have been predisposed to think that because that's a tactic I'd seen in courtrooms. Some lawyers, when confronted with an argument they can't refute, try to trick the jury by twisting the argument into something else. Some politicians are masters of that deception.

However, I may have been wrong to think advocates for atheism are deliberately trying to deceive others about Pascal's point. I now suspect many of them have turned their own mind's eye away from the fly in their atheistic soup.

That said, however, I was a bit disappointed in Pascal's essay myself. He stopped short of conveying an important point. His so-called "wager" may not constitute evidence, but it can lead to evidence. Living as if there is a God will result in a different life experience, and that experience can become evidence.

Experience as Evidence

After formulating the scientific method, Francis Bacon said the best evidence is still experience. Albert Einstein said, "Only experience is knowledge; all else is information." And we all say, "Experience is the best teacher," and "There is no substitute for experience."

In case you're wondering, Professor, I've studied epistemology and theories about how we come to believe what we think we know. I've read that many people stopped thinking of science itself as an exact science after the publication of Thomas Kuhn's *The Structure of Scientific Revolution*. And many years ago I read armchair intellectual works on all sides of the God debate, including some by A. J. Ayer, John Dewey, Sören Kierkegaard, Immanuel Kant, David Hume, René Decartes, and others.

Whew.

If studying that kind of literature is the only way to get at the truth about God, only a few scholars will ever find it. Some philosophers seemed to think they had captured the entire ocean of truth in the teacups of their minds. At the other extreme were those who refused to commit to anything until they were absolutely sure of everything. Regarding the latter, William James asked, "Objective evidence and certitude are doubtless very fine ideals to play with, but where on this moonlit and dream-visited planet are they found?"[85]

After all that reading I circled back to something everyone already knows. Many of our most important beliefs are derived from our own experience. I've read personal testimonies by scientists telling about their faith in God. In many cases their faith was based more on inner experience than on external evidence.[86]

> We all gain much of our knowledge through the "act as if" method—acting as if something is true before we know it is.

William James (1842–1910) was a medical doctor, psychologist, and Harvard professor. He pointed out that we all gain much of our knowledge through the "act as if" method—acting as if something is true before we know it is. Of course that approach is used in scientific experiments, but it is also a natural pattern in everyday life—experiment, experience, evidence, in that order. We act as if something is true and it works, so it becomes part of our belief system. That is the *only way to prove* some things, as reflected by the common expressions, "You'll have to find out for yourself," and "Try it; you'll like it." We all learn some of the most important and pleasurable facts of life by acting as if they are true.

I once heard a man tell of how he stood in a Vietnam battlefield during a rainstorm, shook his fist at the sky, and shouted at God, "You [expletive], I dare you to strike me dead, right now!" His buddies scattered like cockroaches to get away from him. I suppose you could call that an act-as-if experiment to prove God does *not* exist. In any event, it didn't convince him there is no God—at least not permanently. He's an Episcopal priest today.

Kinds of Faith

You, Professor, say, "Faith is an evil precisely because it requires no justification and brooks no argument."[87] Surely you know that is not the only kind of faith there is. The kind of faith I'm talking about begins like a scientific experiment. Sam Shoemaker (1893–1963) explained it like this:

> [Another] thing that helps us find faith is to begin the spiritual experiment in our own lives. You begin it exactly like you begin an experiment in physics or chemistry. You hear that if you mix two ingredients, a certain result will happen. You try it for yourself. If you are seeking a discovery that has not been made, you must take some hypothesis as being true, act as if it were true, and see what happens.[88]

That's the kind of faith I'm urging you to consider. I will offer some specific suggestions for such an experiment in my next letter. Then I'll tell you how it worked out for me. I can anticipate your knee-jerk reaction, Professor. You summarily reject all accounts of faith based on personal experience.[89] But the examples you give are bizarre accounts of visions and far-fetched miracles. As you'll see, that's not what I'll be talking about. Besides, how can you possibly know another person's religious experience isn't real? The great psychiatrist Dr. Carl Jung (1875–1961) said:

> Religious experience is absolute. It is indisputable. You can only say that you have never had such an experience, and your opponent will say: "Sorry, I have." And there your discussion will come to an end. No matter what the world thinks about religious experience, the one who has it possesses the great treasure of a thing that has provided him with a source of life, meaning, and beauty and that has given a new splendor to the world and to mankind. . . . We must, therefore, take them as we experience them.[90]

The Unanswerable Questions

If you ask some people why they believe in God, they won't mention their experience. They prefer to talk about something less personal. So they respond with the question: How did the universe come into existence if there is no God?

As you know, Professor, that question has spawned a chain of arguments that could fill a huge library (including your book, of course). But the crux of many of those arguments can be summarized in this short conversation:

Believer: The universe could not have created itself, so it must have been created by God.

Atheist: But if that's true, who created God?

Believer: God has always existed.

Atheist: Well, maybe the universe has always existed.

Believer: That hypothesis was rejected by scientists when they discovered the universe is expanding at an accelerating rate, so it must have had a beginning they now call the big bang. And even if you could prove the universe has always existed, that wouldn't explain how life began.

Atheist: Evolution explains how life might have begun.

Believer: No, it doesn't. The theory of evolution purports to describe how living things have changed over time, not how life came from nonliving matter in the first place.

Atheist: Even though we don't know how life began, some scientists say that it might have been created when lightning struck some kind of "primordial soup."

Believer: That's so nonspecific it doesn't really say anything—and it's pure speculation. The lightning would have had to keep striking that "soup" with the same result a zillion or so times, until it "somehow" created some cells that could reproduce themselves without help from the lightening.

Atheist: But some scientists say they have made artificial life.

Believer: The key word there is "artificial."

Atheist: Well, scientists have identified the chemical ingredients of life, and say life must have resulted from a mysterious interaction among them.

Believer: That's like saying a barn got built from a mysterious interaction between a stack of lumber and a barrel of nails. After you identify the chemical components of living things, you still have to explain how those nonliving chemicals became the first living cell, and how that first living cell became many living cells, and how those living cells learned to replicate themselves, and then how they learned to produce more complex forms of life. Scientists now know that each living cell results from instructions received from incredibly tiny DNA molecules that contain seemingly infinite amounts of information. *Where did all that information come from?*

That last question reminds me of your conversation with Ben Stein, Professor, in his documentary movie *Expelled.* You acknowledged there may have been a "designer" with a "higher intelligence from elsewhere in the universe" who "seeded" our planet with the first self-replicating molecules that led to life as we know it.

Why won't you call that "designer" with a "higher intelligence" God? The former atheist Antony Flew finally did. In fact he said, "The only satisfactory explanation for the origin of such 'end-directed, self-replicating' life as we see on earth is an infinitely intelligent Mind."[91]

Now let's conclude that conversation by giving Atheist the last word:

> Atheist: Even if we atheists can't give provable—or even plausible—answers to all your questions, such as how the universe and life began, that doesn't prove God exists. Just as no one can lift every object their hands can touch, no one can answer every question their minds can ask. It has been said that even fools can ask questions wise men cannot answer. But those questions that we atheists can't answer don't prove anything. *Unanswered questions are just that—questions, not answers.*

Why do you atheists turn your back on that reasoning when believers can't answer all *your* questions, such as, "Why does God allow suffering?"

The Suffering Question

In a TV interview soon after the terrible events of 9/11, Billy Graham was asked, "Why did God let this happen?" Graham said, "I don't know." In 2011, on the first Good Friday following the devastating tsunami in Japan, Pope Benedict XVI made a television appearance to answer questions from ordinary people. A little girl asked him why God allowed children to suffer in such natural calamities.

The pope said he asked himself that same question and admitted he doesn't have the answer.

Mother Teresa received the Nobel Peace Prize in 1979 for comforting thousands of suffering people, one at a time. It is said that she was once asked what her first words to God would be when she arrived in Heaven. She said, "I will say to Him, 'You have a lot of explaining to do.'"

When believers admit they don't know why God allows suffering, you atheists act as if that settles the issue. But you're making an unspoken assumption that would sound ridiculous if you said it out loud. You're presupposing that if believers were right they could read God's mind and explain why God doesn't do everything we want. But when you can't answer a believer's question—such as how the universe and life began—you take the position that unanswered questions don't prove anything, one way or another.

Nevertheless, I won't end this discussion there. I realize the question of suffering is the most common reason for honest doubts about God. So I want to say a little more about how I dealt with it.

While looking for the answer in books, I noticed that some religious writers dodge the real question. They change it to something like this: "Where is God when you're in pain?" And they say God is right there with you. I've come to believe that's true, but that's not what doubters are asking. They want to know why God allowed the pain in the first place.

I once bought a book by a famous Christian because the title implied he would explain why God allows suffering. But it turned out to be a bait-and-switch title. In the first few pages he just tried to shame the reader for daring to question God. He didn't seem to realize that the Bible itself contains dozens of examples where people asked why God allows suffering.[92] Besides, we don't always *choose* to ask that question. It can just naturally come to mind when bad things happen.

In any event, I will not dodge the question or apologize for asking it. Nor will I pretend to have a comprehensive one-size-fits-all answer. But I will explain why the suffering question no longer stands between me and a belief in God.

One explanation I've heard many times is that everyone deserves to suffer because everyone has sinned. That provokes me to ask, "What sins were committed by a newborn baby with painful birth defects?" Joanie and I have volunteered at a camp for kids with spina bifida. To say those kids deserved to be born that way is beyond absurd.

Another partial explanation for *some* suffering does seem plausible to me. It's based on the fact that we have the power of choice. As a lawyer I've known people who refused to accept any responsibility for the conse-quences of their own bad decisions. They always blamed others, including God. They reminded me of an Old Testament proverb: "A man's own folly ruins his life, yet his heart rages against the Lord."[93] But that's not a complete answer. It doesn't account for natural disasters like earthquakes and tornados.

> We want an obedient God just as children want obedient parents.

I can easily understand why the no-God argument based on suffering has strong emotional appeal. If we assume God could stop all suffering, but chooses not to, that can make us angry. As mentioned earlier, we want an obedient God just as children want obedient parents.

Perhaps it would be more accurate to say that we, like children, want God to be a genie who must grant our wishes. And our first wish would be for God to do away with all the things that make suffering possible.

Or would it?

Let's convert that wish to a prayer and call it "The Prayer to End all Prayers."

God, please take away . . .

our ability to make choices,
for some of our choices cause us grief,

and our ability to remember the past,
because some of our memories are unpleasant,

and our ability to imagine the future,
as that enables us to worry,

and our capacity to know right from wrong,
for that can make us feel guilty,

and our capacity to love others,
as that enables us to feel their pain
and to feel bad when they don't love us.

And kill our curiosity before it kills us.

And while you're at it,
you might as well take away our sex drive,
because it leads to all kinds of trouble.

Wait! Stop! Please, God, disregard all that.
If you granted those wishes,
we'd be subhuman.
We couldn't even pray.

So, God, instead of changing human nature,
change Mother Nature.
Rearrange the natural laws of the universe
from one minute to the next,
enough to accommodate our every
whim and wish.

Suspend the law of gravity,
when we fall, and—

On second thought, please don't do that.
Everything would fly apart.

Oh well, God, You figure it out.
Just make us happy.
Permanently.
All the time.

Then we won't need to pray.

It's easy to say we want God to eradicate everything that makes suffering possible—*unless we get specific about it*. That would include our abilities to make choices, remember the past, imagine the future, know right from wrong, love someone besides ourselves, be curious enough to discover and invent things, and enjoy sex.

As Carl Jung observed, "Every good quality has its bad side."[94] Things that lead to suffering also make it possible to live useful and happy lives. Nobody wants to give up the qualities that make us human, even though they give us both pleasure and pain.

> It's easy to say we want God to eradicate everything that makes suffering possible—unless we get specific about it.

A Life Without Pain was a TV documentary about a little five-year-old girl named Gabby.[95] She suffered from an extremely rare disorder called congenital insensitivity to pain. She had a sense of touch but could feel no pain. By the time Gabby was three years old she had been hospitalized many times due to injuries resulting from her insensitivity to pain. She was blind in one eye from sticking a finger in it.

Not being able to feel pain may sound like a blessing, but it's a devastating disability. That is why Dr. Paul Brand led a project to invent devices to create artificial pain—warning signals. His patients had Hansen's disease, better known as leprosy.[96] Contrary to a common misconception, leprosy doesn't cause pain; it kills it. It numbs pain sensors in the hands, feet, and other extremities, as well as in the eyes. One of Dr. Brand's patients was blind because he didn't realize he was washing his face and eyes with scalding water. Many victims of leprosy are missing fingers and toes because they didn't feel cuts or burns that then became infected.

In his efforts to find substitutes for pain, Dr. Brand found that buzzers and flashes of light were not sufficient. Even electric shocks proved to be inadequate. He eventually abandoned the project.

On many occasions pain has been my friend. I might have died from appendicitis if I hadn't felt a persistent pain in my side. I once used a welding torch without an adequate eye shield. Later that evening the searing pain in my eyes forced me to seek medical help, not only to reduce the pain but to save my eyesight.

It's easy to see why Dr. Brand said, "Thank God for pain."

Some atheists say that if there were a God there would be no pain. On the other hand, some say God should allow children like Gabby to feel pain. To escape this conundrum some atheists say God would have enacted different laws of nature to make pain unnecessary and impossible. So let's consider that.

Why Didn't God "Enact" Different Laws of Nature?

Many people talk about "natural laws" as if they were like laws enacted by a parliament or Congress. But natural laws are nothing like that. When we say the laws of nature were enacted and can be amended, we don't really know what we're talking about. Exactly how, for example, would God repeal or amend the "law" of gravity? Scientists don't yet understand what gravity is.

I once had a philosophy professor who asked the class, "Can God make a square circle?"

One student said, "Yes, God can do anything."

"What does a square circle look like?" the professor asked.

"God only knows," the student said with a smirk.

Then the professor asked the classic question: "Can God make an object so heavy that even he can't lift it?"

That stymied the student because either a yes or no answer would admit there's something God can't do.

The professor was just playing word games, but to make a point. When we put the words "God can" in front of nonsense, it's still nonsense. And it may be nonsense to say different laws of nature could have been "enacted." So maybe Rabbi Harold Kushner was on the right track in his book *When Bad Things Happen to Good People*. He suggested that not even God can stop all suffering.[97] Even though Kushner based his view on passages in the Bible, some religious people called it heresy. They were taught from childhood that God, *by definition*, can do anything, even the logically impossible. But God doesn't have to conform to human dictionaries.

I'm not at all sure Kushner was right. But we don't have to be sure he was right to reject an unspoken assumption made by atheists—that there is no *plausible* way to explain why a loving God would allow bad things to happen. Kushner's view is at least plausible enough to negate that assumption.

To summarize, I can't imagine how God could have "enacted" different laws of nature. So I can't imagine how God would eliminate all the causes of suffering without destroying human nature and Mother Nature in the process. But my inability to imagine such things doesn't prove anything except that there are limits to my imagination.

Come to think of it, I can't imagine why I care about the suffering of others if there is no God.

I don't want to conclude this discussion on suffering without passing along a suggestion I once heard from a clergyman: "If a friend has just experienced the devastating loss of a loved one, go to them and say, 'I am so sorry,' and then *shut up*. In those circumstances," he said, "I am often asked, 'Why did God let this happen?' I always say, 'I don't know,' and continue to console them. That's no time to speculate about the mind of God and the rules of nature."

The Invisible God

Even children know there's more to this world than meets the eye. A class of fifth graders can make a list of things we know exist but cannot see. We can't see those zillions of messages flowing between wireless devices like cell phones. We can't see the force that makes a magnet work. We can't see our own thoughts or feelings, but they drive everything we do. We can't see air, and if we could, wouldn't it obscure our view of everything else?

Astrophysicists tell us that everything we can see makes up less than 5 percent of what exists. And they say there is no such thing as empty space—it's filled with light waves and dark energy (which sounds like a contradiction to me). I have a friend who majored in physics and earned a PhD in mathematics. He says, "I can't see gravity, but I feel its influence. The same is true of God."

One of the most inspiring people of all time, Helen Keller, never claimed she could see or hear God—or anything else. She was totally blind and deaf. Yet her autobiography, *The Story of My Life*, reveals that she sensed the existence of a Supreme Being before she was told about God. That brings to mind an Old Testament verse that refers to God's voice as a "gentle whisper."[98] Maybe that is why so many agnostics and skeptics keep searching. Maybe that is why, as Shakespeare might have said, some atheists protest too much.[99]

When I was a child I asked my father, "Does outer space have a boundary, and if it does, what's on the other side if it's not more space?" Dad explained that our finite minds can't grasp the idea of a universe with or without boundaries—but that doesn't prove or disprove either possibility. He also said there may be some other possibility that is beyond the boundaries of our minds. Sure enough, some physicists later came up with a theory that space is a curved and closed system. I have no idea what that means, but that doesn't prove they're wrong.

People on both sides of the God debate ask questions that people on the other side can't answer. But that does not prove which side is right. Just as atheists admit they can't prove God doesn't exist, I admit that I can't prove why God allows bad things to happen.

Everything is a mystery beyond some point—from the insides of our amazing brains to the outermost boundaries

> Astrophysicists tell us that everything we can see makes up less than 5 percent of what exists.

(if there are any) of the universe. The most complex object discovered thus far is the human brain. Yet it doesn't fully understand itself. If we refused to believe in anything until we had all the answers about it, we would never believe in anything. We would never make a decision because we can never know all the relevant facts or be certain of the outcome. We would never take a job, marry, have children, trust a friend, or walk across a street, much less drive a car down a busy highway. Every minute of every day, we act on faith.

All this leads us back to an obvious fact of life: *many of our most important beliefs can only be learned from personal experience, and much of that experience is gained by acting as if something is true before we know it is.*

"Proofs" of God

You may have noticed that I haven't made some of the older, classic arguments for God's existence. The fact is, Professor, I share your opinion that some of those arguments are not convincing. For example, I just don't get the ontological argument made by Saint Anslem. Trying to understand it almost twists my brain into a pretzel. It goes like this: God is that which nothing greater than can be conceived. If you say God exists only in our heads, then you're not talking about God because something that really exists is obviously greater than that which only exists in our heads. Therefore, when you say "God" you must be talking about something that really exists.[100]

That sounds like a word game to me. In any event, it's not based on what really matters—*personal experience.*

So I don't have a problem, Professor, when you reject certain arguments for God's existence. But I have a huge problem if you mean to imply that a bad argument proves the opposite of its conclusion. Even a bad argument can come to a correct conclusion, albeit for a wrong reason. You, as a scientist, are surely aware of a famous example of this: Galileo said his theory of the earth's dual rotation (on its own axis and around the sun) was proved by the way the tides sloshed up on the shores. He was wrong about what caused the tides, but he was correct about the dual rotation of the earth. The same could be said of a flawed argument for God's existence.

Some arguments for God were thought up by people who already believed in God for another reason. Asking someone why they believe in God can be like asking a happily married couple why they are in love. They may not be able to explain it, but they try to come up with an intelligent sounding answer anyway. The husband might say, "We think alike." The wife may roll her eyes and say, "Opposites attract." The fact remains that they can be in love even if they can't explain why.

Many things can be experienced but not explained. That's why we sometimes say, "Just try it; you'll like it." I've been where you are, Professor. I finally quit trying to find the truth about God by sitting in a chair reading arguments. I got up and tried the practical experiment of living as if God exists. As you'll see in another letter, that proved to be a breakthrough.

Burden of Proof

Most arguments by atheists come down to this: "Nobody has proven to me God exists." Let's assume (for this discussion) that is true. The former atheist Antony Flew finally concluded that scientific facts *do* prove the existence of a Creator. But let's assume (again, for this discussion) the evidence he cited falls short of absolute proof. Let's even go a step further and assume for the moment that it's not even possible for anyone to prove *to another person* that God exists.

That doesn't mean you can't prove it to yourself. There are many things in life you must find out from your own experience. *You can't shift the burden of proving those things to anyone else.*

You have been honest enough, Professor, to acknowledge you can't prove God does *not* exist. Why not see if you can prove God *does* exist? That's something you can attempt by personal experiment in faith. Your refusal to try the experiment may prove something about you, but it will never prove anything about God.

A Secondhand Faith

Some atheists say they did try the God experiment, but it didn't work. An interesting example is Christopher Hitchens, whom I once had the pleasure of meeting in person. He said he became an atheist before the age of ten. However, he seems to have vacillated after that because he says in his book that he was "an Anglican, educated at a Methodist school, converted by marriage to Greek Orthodoxy, recognized as an incarnation by the followers of Sai Baba, and remarried by a rabbi."[101]

My story is a bit less complicated. But I, too, jettisoned the religion of my youth. However, it had been a secondhand faith based on tradition, not a firsthand faith based on experience. In retrospect I can see that's what my religious tradition had urged me to try in the first place. And I had failed to include an essential step that I will discuss in my next letter.

> I, too, jettisoned the religion of my youth. However, it had been a secondhand faith based on tradition, not a firsthand faith based on experience.

Wishing and Believing

People on both sides of the God debate accuse the other of wishful thinking. And they both could be right, at least to some extent.

Some believers say atheists are like spoiled children who want to be free to do whatever they please without regard to moral boundaries. So they become atheists because, as Dostoyevsky said, "If there is no God, anything is permitted." That was obviously the thinking behind those banners for the Atheist Bus Campaign in Britain that said: "There's probably no God. Now stop worrying and enjoy your life."[102] But that slogan is convoluted. Saying there's "probably" no God acknowledges there may be a God. For an atheist that is a cause for concern, not a reason to "stop worrying." And as shown by studies referred to in my first letter, people who believe in God are far more likely to enjoy life than those who don't. So it would make more sense to say, "Choose to believe in God," and *then* say, "Stop worrying and enjoy your life."

Some atheists say believing in God is wishful thinking. Maybe it is sometimes. But the fact that someone wishes something to be true doesn't prove it isn't. Moreover, wishful thinking can be a good thing. Wishful thinking leads to experiments to find cures for cancer. Wishful thinking led Columbus to discover America. Wishful thinking has led to countless act-as-if experiments and many great discoveries.

Of course some act-as-if experiments are bad ideas, as when a little boy jumps off a barn to see if an umbrella works like a parachute. I finally decided against taking the downside risk of living as if there is no God. It makes much better sense to live as if there is a God. The upside possibilities are infinitely better.

A Mountaintop Experience

My son, John, and I have climbed some "fourteeners." That's what they call mountains in Colorado that are over fourteen thousand feet high. Climbing them can be difficult because there is so little oxygen at that altitude. Taking just a few steps can leave you gasping for breath. You suck in all the air you can, but it never seems to be enough. You feel like you're drowning on empty air.

The last fourteener we climbed together was Redcloud Peak in the San Juan mountain range. John, in his forties, could climb faster than I could in my late sixties, so once we were above tree line I urged him to go ahead at his own pace. It didn't take him long to climb over a rise and out of sight.

We had walkie-talkies and I called him an hour or so later. He had already reached the summit. In fact, he was hiking along a ridge on the other side to scale another fourteener about three miles away, Sunshine Peak.

"I'm exhausted," I gasped, "I'm too old for this. I may go back to our campsite."

"Why don't you rest a few minutes," he said, "and then take it slow and easy; it's not so steep near the top, and the view is great."

He was right. The 360-degree panorama was spectacular, a terrific reward for my final push to the summit. So was the feeling of accomplishment. So are the memories.

John had not proved I would be glad if I kept climbing. If I had refused to climb another step unless he proved to me it would be worth the effort, I would have missed the exhilaration of that experience. And John might have attributed my demand for proof to my lightheadedness from the shortage of oxygen.

Now that I believe in God, I naturally want you to have the same experience. But I can't have the experience for you.

All John could do was tell me what he had experienced and encourage me to find out for myself. That's what I'm trying to do in these letters. Now that I believe in God, I naturally want you to have the same experience. But I can't have the experience for you.

The Real Challenge

Ironically, one thing that coaxed me to get on with the faith experiment was the following statement by an agnostic, Herbert Spencer: "There is a principle that is a bar against all information, which is proof against all argument, which cannot fail to keep a man in everlasting ignorance. That principal is contempt prior to investigation."

My next letter will discuss the question: *How* can one go about an experiment in faith?

Sincerely,

Letter No. 3

Regarding Experiments

Dear Professor:
The broadcast journalist Edward R. Murrow said, "The obscure we see eventually; the completely obvious, it seems, takes longer." You may think I took too much time in my last letter pointing out something that is completely obvious—that each of our lives is an almost constant stream of act-as-if experiments. And that is how we learn many of life's most important truths.

This brings us to the question: How can one go about the experiment of living as if there is a God who takes a personal interest in us?

That may seem like a multiple-choice question with a very long list of answers from which to choose. But many of those answers point to the same path, the only differences being a variety of detours into doctrinal issues. One doesn't have to take all those detours to get to the destination. I will discuss what I did about them in another letter. Right now I want to focus on the main path that led me to an unshakable belief in God.

As you will see, the seven steps are pretty basic and very common. I doubt any of them will surprise you.

I will divide the description of the experiment into seven steps. That will make it more orderly than my actual journey, as I went down a few blind alleys. But I won't clutter this letter with all that. I will limit it to those parts of my journey that turned out to be headed in the right direction.

As you will see, the seven steps are pretty basic and very common. I doubt any of them will surprise you.

Three Thinking Steps
Step 1: Admit You Can't Be Certain God Does Not Exist

You've already taken this step, Professor. As previously discussed, you have acknowledged that atheism is an "assumption" you "cannot know for certain" is correct.[103] The atheist S. T. Joshi expressed his frustration with the "impossibility" of proving there is no God.[104]

Step 2: Acknowledge a Personal Need for God

The Scottish scholar William Barclay said, "Without humility there can be no religion, for all true religion begins with a realization of our own weakness and of our need for God."[105] This should be easy for anyone who does not suffer from delusional arrogance. Bruce Sheiman, an atheist author mentioned in my first letter, has been honest enough to say, "I still feel the need for God."[106] Many former atheists, such as C. S. Lewis and Dr. Francis Collins, came to that point before they went on to believe in God.

> William Barclay said, "Without humility there can be no religion, for all true religion begins with a realization of our own weakness and of our need for God."

When measured by the number of people actually helped, Carl Jung (1875–1961) was more effective than Sigmund Freud (1856–1939). In looking back on his career, Jung wrote: "People from all the civilized countries of the earth have consulted me. I have treated many hundreds of patients . . . Among all my patients in the second half of life—that is to say, over thirty-five—there has not been one whose problem in the last resort was not that of finding a religious outlook on life."[107]

Without a religious outlook, I struggled in the quicksand of my own willpower until I crawled out of denial and admitted, "If there is a God, I need His help." Some self-help books were indeed useful, but I finally had to admit that I needed help from a power greater than myself.

That naturally led to the next step.

Step 3: Make a Decision to Try the Faith Experiment

When it appeared England would fall to Hitler, someone asked Churchill if there was any hope America would enter the war. He said, "You can always count on Americans to do the right thing—after they've tried everything else."

I had tried almost everything else before turning to the faith experiment. I finally faced up to the fact that I could spend the rest of my days contemplating arguments about God, only to look back at a squandered life from the dark valley of indecision and regrets. So with nothing to lose and everything to gain, I made the decision to try living as if God exists and see what happened.

As noted in my previous letter, the man who formulated the scientific method said the best evidence is still experience. And the way to gain that experience is to act as if something is true before we know it is. As a science professor you might prefer to call it a working hypothesis. In any case, if you proceed with the faith experiment I believe you will discover the truth in the old saying: "The person with an experience is never at the mercy of someone who merely has an argument."

Step 3 is not an action step, but it is a commitment to take action.

Three Action Steps

The previous steps need to be done only once. The next three should be done every day. This is where the act-as-if experiment really begins.

Step 4: Pray Privately

I asked my friend Preston Bright why he believed in God. He gave several reasons, but the one that intrigued me most was about prayer. He said some of his prayers had been answered in ways he couldn't attribute to coincidence. When I asked him for examples he said, "If I give examples that are not very dramatic, you might suspect they were coincidences. But if I give examples that are dramatic, you would doubt my credibility.

"Besides," he said, "answers to my prayers will never convince you there is a God. Only answers to your own prayers will do that. And you will never have any answered if you don't pray."

I felt strangely hypocritical praying to a God I wasn't sure existed. But that was no more hypocritical than a scientist acting as if some other hypothesis is true.

To be candid, praying is so personal it makes me uncomfortable to talk about it. But I believe praying is an essential part of the experiment, so I feel obliged to at least mention some basic points.

> I felt strangely hypocritical praying to a God I wasn't sure existed. But that was no more hypocritical than a scientist acting as if some other hypothesis is true.

I pray privately. Jesus instructed us to pray "in secret."[108] I pray honestly. At first I acknowledged my doubt: "God, I don't know if you are there, but if you are . . ." I wondered if I was just talking to myself, but that didn't matter as it was an act-as-if experiment.

I pray daily. A model prayer, now called the Lord's Prayer, asks God to "give us today our daily bread."[109] I usually pray in the morning. I ask to be made aware of God's will for me that day, and for the power to carry it out. And I give thanks.

As part of my daily prayer time, I also read some scriptures. One morning I came to this verse in the Old Tes-

> I never did ask for a miraculous sign from God. But I did ask for proof that Jesus was right when he said that those who seek shall find.

tament: "Be still, and know that I am God."[110] So I added a few moments of silence to my morning routine.

I never did ask for a miraculous sign from God. But I did ask for proof that Jesus was right when he said that those who seek shall find.[111] As you'll see in my next letter, that prayer was answered.

Step 5: Live by the Master Rule, Including Worldly Charity

The other steps are mostly about what God can do for us. This is the only one that requires us to do something for others. Without this step the experiment would be an attempt to treat God as a genie whose main purpose is to grant our wishes.

This step is based on what I'm calling the "Master Rule" because all other moral rules are derived from it. Jesus said it "sums up the Law and the Prophets."[112] Hindus call it "the sum of duty."[113] Rabbi Hillel said that once you have heard this rule "all the rest is commentary."[114]

The Master Rule has been expressed in various ways, but it comes down to this: *treat others as you would be treated in their circumstances.*

Of course this is more commonly called the Golden Rule. I didn't want to call it that because some readers might have shrugged it off as a platitude. But it is *not* just a platitude. It is the most profound and practical moral guideline ever conceived. Just think how much better the world would be if everyone obeyed it and how much worse it would be if nobody did.

I would like to keep calling it the Master Rule, but that might be a distraction. It has been called the Golden Rule at least since the 1670s, when it was also referred to as the "Golden Law."

Versions of the Golden Rule are found in Christianity, Hinduism, Buddhism, Judaism, Islam, Bahá'í, Brahmanism, Confucianism, Jainism, Scientology, Shinto, Sikhism, Taoism, and Zoroastrianism.[115] It often gets buried under layers of religious rhetoric, but if you drill through all that to the bedrock teachings of almost any religion, you will find it there.

I wonder how the Golden Rule got into so many religions before they could have all learned it from each other. The atheist Christopher Hitchens said it "is gradually learned, as part of the painfully slow evolution of the species."[116] But he didn't mention any fossil remains or other evidence to support that statement. It's just as reasonable to assume it came from a common source: God.

Hitchens also said atheists can comply with the Golden Rule just like anyone else. But he said an advantage of being an atheist is that you don't have to be concerned when you don't.[117] Perhaps he should have called it the Golden "Option." It's no surprise that studies referred to in my first letter show that atheists are not nearly as likely to abide by the Golden Rule as people of faith are.

Some religions express the Golden Rule in positive terms (*do* unto others what you would want done unto you) while others put it in negative terms (do *not* do unto others what you would *not* want done to you). This difference can be important when determining certain legal obligations and liabilities. But it makes no difference in commonsense moral applications. If you see a starving child, the positive version tells you to give food to the child. The negative version tells you not to withhold food from the child. But both versions are saying, *Just feed the child*.

That leads us to the most obvious and urgent application of the Golden Rule.

Worldly Charity

The adjective "worldly" signals that we're talking about helping people in need of such basic things as food, water, clothes, and shelter, those who are sick or who have disabilities, or those who need to find ways to lift themselves out of poverty.

As I said earlier, I will explain in another letter why I chose the religion of Jesus for my experiment. I mention it again here because Jesus placed the highest possible emphasis on down-to-earth charity. In no uncertain terms he indicated it is a nonnegotiable requirement.[118] So it's no surprise that Christians provide humanitarian assistance to billions around the world.

Yet I know some Christians who seem to think helping those in need is just an option for bonus points. They pray for the poor and hungry and wish them well, but *do* little or nothing for them. That's not enough according to many passages in the New Testament, such as this one:

> Suppose a brother or sister is without clothes
> and daily food. If one of you says to him, "Go,

I wish you well; keep warm and well fed," but does nothing about his physical needs, what good is that? In the same way, faith by itself, if it is not accompanied by action, is dead.[119]

This passage doesn't say faith without works is weak. It says faith without works is *dead*. Another part of the same passage says a person is made right with God by what he does, and "not by faith alone." But another passage says a person is saved by God's "grace . . . through faith" and "not by works."[120]

I once heard a Baptist preacher explain why these passages are not inconsistent. He said they are talking about two different kinds of faith: (1) a passive intellectual acceptance of factual teachings *about* the Lord, and (2) an active commitment to obey the moral teachings *of* the Lord. He said the first without the second is not enough. Likewise, Billy Graham said that the kind of faith God requires is a "total commitment," not just "intellectual acceptance."[121] It can be compared to putting your "faith" in a heart surgeon. That's not just a belief that the surgeon exists and has a medical license. Putting "faith" in the surgeon is a commitment to do what the surgeon tells you to do and to trust him to do what he says he will do. Just *saying* you have faith in the surgeon won't fix your heart. Jesus made it clear that lip service isn't enough for God either.[122] C. S. Lewis said that from real faith "good actions must inevitably come," so the old faith-or-works argument is "like asking which blade in a pair of scissors is most necessary."[123] One without the other won't cut it. We might as well argue over whether it is more important to breathe out or to breathe in. The argument itself is a waste of breath. If you don't do both, you're dead. Likewise, the kind of faith that doesn't result in charitable actions is dead.

That preacher said we cannot do enough good works to save ourselves, so God's grace is required. But saying works are not enough does not mean no works are necessary. That would be like saying water is not enough to keep us alive, so water is not necessary to keep us alive. I'm no theologian, but that preacher made sense to me. In any event, I find it impossible to read the words of Jesus and think he regarded worldly charity as anything less than a firm requirement. And charity is most definitely an important application of the Golden Rule as found in all major religions.

In retrospect I can see the main reason the faith of my youth didn't survive. I had professed a belief in certain teachings *about* Jesus, but had not made an unconditional commitment to obey the teachings *of* Jesus. And those teachings require worldly charity.[124]

I recently heard a young preacher speak as if the obligation to engage in charity is limited to a chosen few with a "spiritual gift" for it. I imagined some teenager in the congregation thinking, *Great! I can stop feeling guilty about not helping the poor and needy. That's not my gift. Neither is cleaning my room or doing homework.*

Many charitable organizations need volunteers to perform tasks that do *not* require any special talents. And some train their volunteers.

On the other hand, some charities do need help from people with unique talents and skills. My wife Joanie is a gifted artist. Her paintings sell for thousands of dollars and she donates all her proceeds to charities for children.

As a volunteer she has taught arts and crafts to hundreds of kids with disabilities. But one teenager she taught demonstrated the fact that you don't need a natural ability to help others. He had cerebral palsy and used a battery-powered wheelchair. That didn't prevent him from finding ways to encourage others. He inspired me so much I wrote an article about him.[125] Many people with disabilities do charity work.

I've heard some people say charity work is not their "calling." That means they're not in the mood to do it. I'm always tempted to tell them something I say to my students: "Don't waste your life waiting on the right mood." At the beginning of my course on leadership I hand out this quote from Thomas Huxley: "Perhaps the most valuable result of all education is the ability to make yourself do the thing you have to do, when it ought to be done, whether you like it or not."

I've heard some people say charity work is not their "calling." That means they're not in the mood to do it.

I must confess that I only dabbled in charity work at first, mostly for social and business reasons. I increased my donations of money to charities, but that was easy as I had a good income. I was shamed into giving more when I learned that the working poor in the US give a higher percentage of their incomes to charities than the middle class and wealthy.[126] I also read the passage where Jesus praised a poor widow who gave very little, but more than everyone else in terms of how much she had.[127]

However, when it came to volunteering significant amounts of *time*, I kept putting it off. My excuse was that I worked very long hours and most weekends. I finally faced up to the fact that I had to force some volunteer charity work into the experiment. That required teeth-clenching determination. I worked on some houses for Habitat for Humanity on weekends. That was a great experience. A life-changing breakthrough came when I took a one-week vacation to go with Joanie to Camp John Marc (described in my first letter). We worked in the camp for kids with spina bifida. That turned out to be one of the most gratifying things I've ever done. So I signed up to do it every year.

Excuses for Not Practicing Charity

Some say we shouldn't help those who can and should be helping themselves because it rewards them for being lazy and irresponsible, which, in the long run, does them more harm than good. I won't wade into that issue here except to say it's not a valid excuse for not practicing *any* charity. There is no shortage of people who desperately need help they can't provide for themselves.

Another common excuse for not practicing charity goes like this: "The needs are so great anything I do will be like throwing a few buckets of water on a forest fire. So why bother?"

That's a fair question. But it's not rhetorical. There is an answer. Jesus told a parable about a lost sheep that reminds us we must sometimes focus all our attention on just one.[128] After all, that's what *you* are—a one. *Well, so is everyone else.*

Imagine you are in an emergency room suffering severe chest pains and struggling for breath. But the doctors on duty are just standing there with their arms folded, looking unconcerned. One says, "There must be hundreds of people having heart attacks right now. We can't save them all. So why bother to save this one?"

Bill Moyers reminds us, "Our very lives depend on the ethics of strangers, and most of us are always strangers to other people."

One of the most famous short stories ever told is about a man who helped a stranger. The published version of the story doesn't give the hero's name, so let's call him Sam. Sam saw an injured man on the ground beside a path. He had been beaten and robbed. Two very religious men just walked by him without offering to help. Sam was a member of a class of people those religious men regarded as inferior. But he stopped to help the man. After caring for the man's wounds, Sam took him to an inn for the night. (In those days inns sometimes served as the functional equivalent of hospitals.) He paid the innkeeper and promised to return and pay any additional expenses.

We now call Sam the Good Samaritan.

Do you recall the question that prompted Jesus to tell that story? You're only half right if you said, "Who is my neighbor?" That was a follow-up question. The original question was: "What must I do to receive eternal life?" (Notice the word "must" in that question.) Jesus told him to obey the commandment to love God and to love your "neighbor" as you love yourself. Hoping to limit the scope of the commandment, the man asked Jesus what the word "neighbor" meant. Jesus told that parable about helping a total stranger and said, "Go and do likewise."[129]

Below are some charitable organizations alongside phrases patterned after the passage where Jesus said that whatever we do for others we do for him.[130]

When I needed food: Meals on Wheels
When I needed water: Water for People
When I needed clothes: The Salvation Army
When I needed shelter: Habitat for Humanity
When I was lonely: Alzheimer's Association
When I was in prison: Prison Fellowship Ministries
When I was sick: Leukemia & Lymphoma Society
When I was blind: National Federation of the Blind
When I was crippled: March of Dimes Birth Defects
  Foundation
When I was poor: Goodwill Industries International

A complete list of charitable organizations that need donations and volunteers would fill volumes. A list of people who need their help would seem endless. But each and every one of those people is a "one" just like you.

Another Major Application of the Golden Rule: Forgiveness.

Jesus said, "If you do not forgive men their sins, your Father will not forgive your sins."[131]

Forgiveness has been defined as letting go of resentments. Over a thousand published studies show that *not* letting go of resentments has "specific physiologic consequences—such as increased blood pressure and hormonal changes—linked to cardiovascular disease, immune suppression and, possibly, impaired neurological function and memory."[132]

Revenge may seem sweet in movies, but in real life it is emotional poison.[133] Dr. Dean Ornish said, "In a way, the most selfish thing you can do for yourself is to forgive other people."[134]

It's easy to say we should "let go" of resentments. But how can we do it? It helped me to realize that forgiveness is not pretending to forget what someone did. Nor is it being naïve by trusting them not to do it again. Letting go of a resentment begins with a decision not to do anything for the purpose of "getting even" with them. It's not denying that you have a natural *desire* to get revenge. It's choosing not to act on that desire. Once that decision is made, the resentment begins to lose its control over us.

Of course there can be other reasons to take action to prevent a recurrence of the offense. And that action can be consistent with the Golden Rule, which tells us how to treat "others." There may be multiple "others" to consider. A common example is when an employee persists in being rude to customers notwithstanding warnings to change his attitude. To fire him may comply with the Golden Rule regarding those who depend on the business for their livelihoods. But the employer can still let the employee go in a compassionate way. I've seen businesses incur huge legal costs as a result of failing to do that.

I found it easy to forgive close friends and members of my immediate family. But I found it hard to forgive others who obviously didn't regret what they did and would do it again if given half a chance. Yet I knew that hanging on to resentments interfered with my own peace of mind, usually without affecting theirs.

Forgiveness has been aptly if not elegantly described as an emotional laxative.

Negative Applications of the Golden Rule

I once heard a speaker at a seminar for lawyers say, "The Golden Rule is a fine general guideline, but it would be tragic if everyone always followed it." He gave the example of a mother who lets her child play in a busy street if that's what the child wants to do.

The speaker assumed the Golden Rule requires us to let others do whatever they wish regardless of the consequences. But that's ridiculous. Imagine you see a little girl about to run across a street into the path of a bus she doesn't see coming. You save her life by grabbing her collar and pulling her back, accidentally ripping her jacket in the process. That might seem like a violation of the Golden Rule for an instant. But of course it's just the opposite. The same is true when a parent won't allow a child to play in the street.

When a child becomes a teenager it gets more complicated. As a lawyer I've seen terrible things happen when parents have failed to use tough love. One father paid all his son's traffic tickets and never grounded him for getting so many. One night his son was driving too fast, rolled his car, and died as a result of the accident. The grieving father felt he had killed his son with kindness.

On the other hand, tough love can also have horrible consequences, and I have never come up with a one-size-fits-all approach for deciding when to use it. So it would be naïve of me to imply it's always easy to know how to comply with the Golden Rule. We all face moral dilemmas.

Nevertheless, the Golden Rule is the best moral compass there is, even when it's hard to be sure where it's pointing.

Other Applications

Complying with the Golden Rule can be to pay a compliment, let another driver into traffic, or leave a generous tip for a waitress. Another way is to be loyal to friends who are not present. I've heard too much nasty gossip introduced with these words: "We need to pray for her because . . ."

One profoundly important application of the Golden Rule is to *listen*—not just to permit someone to talk, but to really focus on what they are saying and feeling. While practicing law, I was a good listener as that was essential to my success. But in most other roles I have to work at it.

I have only touched on a few ways to comply with the Golden Rule—worldly charity, forgiveness, tough love, common courtesies, being loyal to friends who are absent, and listening to those who are present. You can doubtless think of many more. In any event, nothing is more vital to the experiment than a fiercely determined effort to treat others as you would be treated in their circumstances.

The next step concerns the other side of the coin— how to treat yourself.

Step 6: Be Good to Yourself, Too

Some people talk about the Golden Rule as if it means we're supposed to be human doormats, always placing our own welfare beneath that of others. But it says to treat

> The test question for being good to ourselves is not, "Will this make me feel good right now?" It is, "Will this make me feel good about myself later?"

others "as" we would be treated, not better than. A doctor friend put it like this: "I can't help my patients by catching their diseases. To serve them I need to follow my own advice and take care of myself."

When I was a child I heard a shouting preacher say we should loathe ourselves because we are all sinners. But later I read where Jesus called the following Hebrew Scripture one of the two greatest commandments: "Love your neighbor as yourself."[135] It occurred to me that if God wants us to love others as much as we love ourselves, it follows that we're supposed to love ourselves as much as God wants us to love others. Moreover, the word "love" as used in that commandment is not a noun for an affectionate feeling. It is a verb, an *action* word. That means we should be good to ourselves. This applies to our physical, mental, emotional, social, financial, and spiritual well-being.

The test question for being good to ourselves is not, "Will this make me feel good right now?" It is, "Will this make me feel good about myself later?"

This step may require us to get help from someone else. I've had the pleasure of seeing friends and clients overcome serious personal problems—including addictions, depression, and financial difficulties—by getting professional help and joining support groups. After all, if God wants us to give help it must be OK to receive it.

This step tells us what kind of God to assume exists when we begin the act-as-if experiment—a God who loves us and wants us to do the same.

Now let's move on to the seventh step.

A Communal Step

Steps 1–4 can be private matters. Steps 5 and 6 may result in some improvements in your behavior that others will appreciate, but you don't have to tell them a religious experiment has anything to do with it.

The next step may require a little courage because it is clearly religious and must be done in public.

Step 7: Join Others on the Journey

I had to swallow some false pride to take this step. I had vowed never to go back to church except for weddings and funerals. But most of my excuses made no more sense than saying I'll never eat another vegetable because:

- My parents made me eat vegetables when I was a child
- There are too many to choose from
- Some aren't good
- People who sell them just want your money
- Some vegetarians are hypocrites—they have healthier-than-thou attitudes but sneak around and eat meat

However, my main criticism of churches concerned their budgets. I felt they didn't spend enough on worldly charity. Their members said they gave their tithes and offerings "to God," but the church spent most of it on the church itself and activities for its members, like a country club.

I finally realized a church's budget doesn't reflect all the good it does.

People are inspired at church to donate to organizations like the Salvation Army. Those donations don't show up on church budgets.

> Those who criticize churches from the outside (as I did) may be the real hypocrites (as I was).

People are inspired at church to volunteer for organizations like Habitat for Humanity. The hours they spend doing that don't show up on church budgets.

People who attend church donate significantly more blood than anyone else. Not one drop of that shows up on church budgets.

In short, some churches inspire and practice a lot of charity not reflected on their accounting records. As illustrated in my first letter, studies show that people who go to church give a lot more to charities than people who don't. That's true even if you don't count their donations to the church. They give more to secular charities than secularists. And the more often people attend church, the more they give outside the church.

Therefore, those who criticize churches from the outside (as I did) may be the real hypocrites (as I was).

I recently read a book by a young woman who cites statistics that show a decline in church memberships over the last few decades. She leaps to the conclusion that churches no longer offer what people need. But there has also been a steeper decline in healthy eating habits. Does that prove no grocery stores sell healthy foods? Of course not. Many people join fitness clubs pursuant to New Year's resolutions but stop using them by March. Does that prove those clubs stop providing what those people need? Of course not. It indicates more about the absent members than the clubs. The same is true of many who don't attend church.

Besides, *voluntary* church attendance is not declining as much as the numbers indicate. Before laws were passed against discrimination on religious grounds, getting a job in some communities could be next to impossible if you weren't a member in good standing at a local church. Some banks would not make you a loan unless you listed your pastor as a reference. Peter Drucker put this in perspective when he said: "But what is amazing is not that the churches have lost members, but that they have lost so few! For the church membership of yesterday—and yesterday means only fifty or sixty years ago—was in a good many cases social compulsion rather than free choice."[136]

Millions attend church without being pressured to go. Millions more attend despite being pressured *not* to go. So something worthwhile must be happening in many of them.

A Bad (but Funny) Experience in Church

We lived in Anchorage, Alaska, when I started back to church. At first I attended only the main worship service. Then I decided to attend Sunday school, too, mainly as an example for our preteen son.

Our son went to a class for kids his age while Joanie and I went to a department for married couples. The director pointed to a door and said to me, "The men's class meets in there."

The room had about thirty chairs in it, none of which were occupied. I sat on the front row. I was the only person in the room for several minutes that seemed much longer than they were.

Finally, a tall slender man in his mid-thirties walked in, nodded slightly in my direction, and mumbled, "Good morning." His long black beard surrounded no hint of a smile. He virtually marched to the podium, about five feet in front of me. He opened his Bible and arranged his notes in silence.

He looked around the room as if he were about to deliver a major speech to a large convention.

His audience still consisted of one person—me.

Then he began shouting a diatribe that went on for one of the longest half hours of my life. I would have walked out, but I didn't want to embarrass Joanie.

That obliterated my resolve to attend Sunday school at that church.

Good Experiences in Church

Notwithstanding that incident in Sunday school, I continued going to the worship services. I liked the preacher more than his preaching. He was a "sourdough," a distinction reserved for people who had survived many winters in Alaska. I came to think of his sermons like the keys in my pocket. They don't all fit the same lock, but that doesn't mean any of them are bad keys. When a sermon didn't fit my lock, I figured it might be helping someone else. And now and then he did say something that helped me, such as, "If you want something you don't have, you may have to do something you're not doing." Pretty obvious, but for some reason it connected and caused me to make a significant improvement in my life.

I don't envy ministers for the daunting challenge of trying to think of something new and worthwhile to say week after week, year after year. It's no wonder they don't always get a thumbs-up from all the self-appointed critics in the pews.

Soon after we moved to Dallas, I made an extended business trip back to Alaska. While I was away, Joanie and our son, John, visited a church. They liked it, so we joined after I returned. They couldn't have chosen a better one for me. The senior pastor, Dr. Clyde Fant, was a brilliant scholar, successful author, and great speaker. He spoke on things that really mattered in real life. He and I eventually became close friends. He understood where I was on my journey and was not judgmental. Out of thousands of churches in the Dallas area, "coincidence" had led me to one that was right for me.

At first I was put off by a few self-righteous members and one who was dishonest. But I had to remind myself that all worthwhile institutions attract some fanatics and frauds. And nobody's perfect. So churches, like all human organizations, are filled with imperfect people—including me.

Expressing Doubts at Church

I once saw a newspaper ad showing a man in church with tape over his mouth. The caption read: "Some churches have all the answers because they don't allow all the questions."

> I don't believe a church
> is obligated to provide
> a platform for anyone who
> wishes to challenge the
> reasons for its existence.

I liked that ad when I saw it, but now I have mixed feelings about it.

During a discussion in a Sunday school class at that church in Dallas, I asked a question that challenged a basic tenet in their creed. That obviously disturbed some people. They had been brought up on religious beliefs they had never seriously questioned. They had no reason to question them, as living in accordance with those beliefs was working well for them and their families.

After that I tried to comply with the Golden Rule by refraining from asking questions at church that challenged anyone's faith. Instead I discussed my doubts privately with someone qualified to talk about them.

I don't believe a church is obligated to provide a platform for anyone who wishes to challenge the reasons for its existence. The purpose of a worship service is just that—to worship. Most Sunday school classes are intended to help one learn how to live out one's faith, not to question it. A church is a place to find encouragement and hope, enjoy fellowship, perform marriages, celebrate births, comfort people in grief, and inspire and facilitate efforts to help others in need.

Some churches do provide opportunities for people to deal with doubts about the existence of God. Some invite them to talk privately with someone on the staff. Some hold group sessions for such purposes. Some invite special speakers to address difficult questions. Some distribute books for those who prefer to deal with their doubts privately.

A Tale of Two Apples

When I was six years old an uncle who owned a grocery store gave me a basket of apples. I took a bite of one and spit it out. It was bitter. So I decided I didn't like apples.

Forty years later Joanie and I were on a driving vacation near Flagstaff, Arizona. She bought some apples from a roadside vendor. She said they were delicious and offered one to me. "You know I don't like apples," I said. She insisted, so I took a bite. To my surprise, I loved it.

For four decades I had allowed one bitter bite to deprive me of the pleasure and benefits of eating apples.

Likewise, I let some bad experiences in a few churches turn me off to all churches. Of course that wasn't reasonable because not all churches are alike—not even close.

In retrospect I can see that at least five things led me to include church attendance in the experiment:

- I had fond memories from being active in church as a teenager. I formed some lifelong friendships there. Best of all, that's where I met Joanie. As of the moment I'm writing this sentence, we've been married fifty years and two days.
- Jesus taught that going to church is not something we do for God. It's something God wants us to do for ourselves. We all need to recharge our physical and spiritual batteries.
- Jesus said we must acknowledge our faith commitment publicly.
- Jesus set the example by attending religious services *even though he did not agree with everything he heard there.*
- It just makes sense to spend time with others on the same journey.

Here's one final thought about churches that some readers may need to consider: a friend once told me, "I had to find God in [a Twelve-Step program], but now that I've found Him, I take Him to church with me."

You can spend the rest of your life recycling inconclusive arguments about God. Or you can try the experiment of living as if God exists and see what happens. I hope you will consider the experiment that has been suggested.

Three thinking steps that need to be done only once:
1. Admit you can't be certain God does *not* exist.
2. Acknowledge a personal need for God.
3. Make a decision to try the faith experiment.

Three action steps that should be done every day:
4. Pray privately.
5. Live by the Master Rule, including worldly charity.
6. Be good to yourself, too.

One more step that should be done at least once a week:
7. Join others on the journey.

If you do those things, I believe you will thank God for the outcome. I did, and I'll tell you about that in my next letter.

Sincerely,

Letter No. 4

Regarding Evidence

Dear Professor:

In my last letter I suggested a way to go about an experiment in faith. I'll start this one by telling you how it worked out for me.

The God Racket

I'm not being flippant or sacrilegious when I say God turned out to be like my first oversized tennis racket. Please suspend judgment while I explain.

When I lived in Anchorage, Alaska, a friend built an indoor tennis club. It had enough courts to accommodate a large membership. I signed up for weekly lessons and played most evenings after work and on weekends.

I lost about 90 percent of the time.

Then I saw a magazine advertisement for a new "oversized" racket. At that time (the late 1970s), standard racket faces were about sixty-five square inches. The one in the ad was 110 square inches. I wanted one but they weren't available in local stores yet. In those days a lot of merchandise was shipped to Anchorage by sea, but magazines arrived by air. So we often read about new products long before they could be purchased locally—and we couldn't order them online because the Internet didn't exist.

A few days later I made a business trip to the Lower 48 and bought one. On the return flight I daydreamed about winning matches against players who had always defeated me—and that's exactly what happened. I even won a tournament and was named the most improved player in the club.

A friend, after losing to me for the first time, asked to hold my new racket. He examined it as if searching for an explanation other than the obvious—the larger racket face. Finally he said, "It must be psychological; the ball still only touches the same size area on the strings." He continued studying the racket, and then repeated his opinion, "It's just psychological."

Leo, our club's tennis pro, overheard my friend and said, "Who cares? He's *winning*."

That put the issue to rest so far as I was concerned. I continued to enjoy winning and didn't worry about why the new racket worked.

I felt much the same way when my experiment in faith began to change my life. Whenever I found myself wondering if the underlying cause might be just psychological, I'd think, *Who cares? I'm winning.* My little mustard seed of faith was moving some mountains. My physical exercise program progressed from good intentions to a consistent habit. I lost forty-two pounds (or "three stones" as you British say). I trained for and completed a marathon (26.2 miles) and told a friend, "I ran two marathons on the same day—my first one and my last one." I'm now past seventy and still run half marathons (13.1 miles) for charities. I've won several first place medals in my current age group, 70–74 (usually because I am the only one in that age group).

I also became a better manager of my time, money, and emotions. My temperament improved. While our son was home on furlough from the marines, he asked Joanie, "What's happened to Dad?" She told him it was "something spiritual."

Virtually all my relationships got better. A man who had worked with me for several years told me privately, "Everyone is talking about how you've changed, and they love it." I thanked him and he asked, "What made the difference?" I dodged his question, but was glad to have heard it.

Lest you think I'm bragging, let me assure you I'm no poster boy for religious faith. Hardly a day goes by I don't regret something I've done or failed to do. But I am at worst a lot less bad than I was before. If I were a celebrity I might write an autobiography about the dramatic changes in my life, but suffice it to say I began to win some major battles I'd been losing with godless self-help remedies. I wasn't sure why the experiment was working, but I was deeply grateful that it was.

At that point, if you had asked me if I believed in God I might have said, "For all practical purposes, yes." My glass of faith was about 90 percent full. But I was 100 percent sure my life had profoundly improved, and I never wanted to go back to the way it was.

William James said, "It is wrong always, everywhere, and for everyone, to believe anything upon insufficient evidence." But he also said, "Truth is what works." As a teacher of science, Professor, you have doubtless read about experiments that ended with the exciting words, "It *works*." Those words often precede an understanding of *why* it works. In much the same way, faith works. You don't have to know why. And you don't have to take my word for it. Thousands of studies show that people of faith are likely to be happier and healthier than anyone else.[137] Of course I'm talking about a positive and charitable faith, not the toxic, selfish, and fraudulent kinds you talk about in your book.

At that point you might say I had a functional faith. I was not 100 percent certain of God's existence, but I was certain my life was better. If my faith had never risen above that level I would have remained deeply grateful and never looked back. But it didn't stop there.

Beyond All Doubt

With that new tennis racket, my game continued to improve. I won some more trophies. I still wasn't sure if the real reason was the racket or something psychological.

Then the mystery was solved. A tennis magazine explained the "secrets" of the new oversized racket. The larger "sweet spot," or optimum hitting area, made the racket more forgiving when the ball was hit off-center. And the "trampoline effect" caused the ball to stay on the strings a bit longer, giving more control over its direction. As a result, all tennis rackets became larger, as they are today.

So the improvements in my tennis game had not been just psychological after all. The new racket had actually made a difference.

Likewise, I became convinced God was the real reason the faith experiment was working. My faith began as a commitment, grew into confidence, and became a conviction. There have been moments when my belief in God was involuntary, leaving no room for doubt. At other times I trust the memory of those moments, much as I still believe in the sun at midnight.

Now, Professor, if I said something like that in a public debate you might ask, "Are you saying God has spoken to you?" You atheists love to ask that question. You know it creates a

> There have been moments when my belief in God was involuntary, leaving no room for doubt. At other times I trust the memory of those moments, much as I still believe in the sun at midnight.

no-win situation in front of an audience. If I say no, you will shrug your shoulders to imply, "Well, then, you don't really know God exists." But if I say yes, you will smirk, knowing some in the audience will suspect that I'm delusional.

As a lawyer I am well aware of ways to frame no-win questions. I could respond by saying, "Let me ask you that same question, Professor, about your idol Charles Darwin. Has he ever spoken to you?" That might draw some laughs from the audience since Darwin died before you were born. But that really doesn't get at the kind of experience I'm talking about.

I won't say I've heard an audible, humanlike voice from God or seen a vision. Nor am I talking about an emotional upheaval. I won't say such things don't happen for others. But I'm talking about matter-of-fact moments of just knowing God was there.

One such moment occurred at Camp John Marc, the camp for kids with chronic illnesses and disabilities that I mentioned earlier. Joanie did some artwork for new cabins there, and I joined her at the dedication ceremony. I watched kids enjoy the thrill of speeding down the zip line. I saw their parents trying, unsuccessfully, to hold back tears of gratitude. I thought about the volunteers and sacrificial donations and the sweat, talent, and prayers that created that camp and kept it going. Most of all, I thought about my heroes, the campers. I knew the camp would not exist without people motivated by their religious faith. And I knew I wouldn't be there if I had not tried my own experiment in faith.

At that moment, it happened: I felt an unmistakable

awareness of a loving God. I found it impossible to believe that camp was the accidental result of random collisions of mindless subatomic particles in an unplanned, godless universe.

Most such moments have occurred when I stepped out of my comfort zone to help someone—at Camp John Marc, in Africa while helping administer life-saving vaccines to children, and at a volunteer agency for the blind. Some moments of certainty have come in the form of answered prayers. One came out of the blue during a prayer. Another on the summit of a mountain I climbed with my son. Once, while a choir sang Handel's "Hallelujah Chorus," I thought, *The only explanation for that kind of music is that the God they're singing about inspired it.*

Dr. Clyde Fant, a dear friend and scholar whom I admire and trust, once told me about the experience of a tough, retired career army officer, a lieutenant colonel and a veteran of Korea and Vietnam. He was a skeptic on most religious questions. Nevertheless, he sometimes returned to a place he called his "spiritual home" at a retreat center. One Sunday morning he sat with two of his oldest friends on the floor in the simple wooden chapel called Shantivanam, "Forest of Peace." They were looking toward the pulpit and a large window that looked out on a quiet meadow with woods beyond it. Most of the service was spent in quiet contemplation. As the hour ended, tears were streaming down his face. He turned to a friend and said, "I felt God's Spirit for the first time today."

As you mentioned in your book, Professor, when Dr. Carl Jung was asked if he believed in God he said, "I don't believe in God, *I know* there is a God."[138]

> I found from experience that Jesus was right when he said, "He who seeks finds."

An ancient Greek philosopher said, "It is very difficult to find God, and when you have found Him, it is impossible to tell anyone else about Him." The Apostle Paul said the peace that comes from faith transcends understanding.[139] It can be experienced but not explained.

The atheist-turned-Christian C. S. Lewis said faith is "really finding out by experience that it is true."[140] I found from experience that Jesus was right when he said, "He who seeks finds."[141] I now firmly believe the Hebrew scripture in the Old Testament: "If from there you seek the Lord your God, you will find him if you look for him with all your heart and with all your soul."[142] A key word in those passages is "seek." No one could do that for me. No one can do it for you, either. That is something each of us must do for ourselves.

The Color Delusion

As indicated by the title of your book, *The God Delusion*, you assume no religious experience is genuine if it can't be explained to your satisfaction. How would you feel, Professor, if a blind man accused you of having "a color delusion"? After all, you can't describe colors to someone who has never seen them. I once heard a blind man say, "I've learned to talk about colors but I have no idea what they are."

How can you possibly know another person's religious experience isn't real? Maybe you haven't had one yourself, but that doesn't prove no one else has. Nor does it prove you can't have a similar experience. But no one can have it for you.

Like you, I once suspected no religious experience was genuine if it couldn't be described. But we've all had experiences we can't describe. A human life normally results from an intensely pleasurable sensation that is impossible to describe, especially to someone too young to have had a similar experience.

Visualize a loving mother in a rocking chair holding her baby daughter with a Raggedy Ann doll. You can easily describe the doll, but not the mother's love. Yet her love is infinitely more important than the doll.

To repeat something Dr. Carl Jung said: "Religious experience is absolute. It is indisputable. You can only say that you have never had such an experience, and your opponent will say: 'Sorry, I have.' And there your discussion will come to an end."[143]

Well, it's time for this letter to do just that—come to an end. I leave you with this thought: *you will never have a religious experience by refusing to do what is necessary to have one.*

In my next letter I'll keep my promise to explain why I chose the Christian religion for the experiment.

Sincerely,

John

Letter No. 5

Regarding Christianity

Dear Professor:

I write this letter as a layman with no right to speak for any other Christian, much less for the entire religion. I write only as former skeptic who now believes Jesus was who he said he was.[144] I came to believe that without trying to resolve all the disagreements that divided his religion into many denominations. I will briefly explain what I did about doctrinal disputes in my next letter. In this one I will focus on my original core reasons for turning to the religion of Jesus.

T. S. Eliot said he accepted Christianity because it was the "least false option" available to him. In my case, it was the only option I knew much about. But the main reason for that was the accident of my birthplace. So I began reading about other religions.

I quickly decided not to consider any other religion for the experiment. I'll explain why not, but I'll make it brief.

The Other Religions

I didn't undertake an in-depth study of any religion, much less all of them. I had already read a virtual library on the issue of God's existence. I had no intention of launching another reading expedition into all the world's religions and the countless variations within each one. I couldn't believe God would require that much research to find the way, so I read only a handful of books. Here is a short account of where that left me.

Islam

Islam is the second largest religion. Some Christians are surprised to hear that the Quran says many of the same things about Jesus as the New Testament: that he was born to the Virgin Mary, lived a sinless life, was a Messenger of God, performed many miracles, ascended into heaven, and will return as the Messiah to bring peace to the world.

Nevertheless, it was my impression that Islam was an angry religion. (Later, I made many business trips to an Islamic country over a twenty-year period. I found that I had misjudged the true religion of Islam, just as many Muslims misjudge Christianity based on what some Christians did to Muslims during the Crusades.)

Hinduism

Gandhi said he was strongly influenced by Jesus, and some Hindus believe Jesus was a "God-man."[145] But a Hindu proverb says, "One goal, many paths," meaning many religions lead to the right place. That reminded me of those directories in shopping malls with an arrow pointing to a spot on the map with the notation, "You are here." So

Hinduism seemed to say, "Start from where you are, and if that is in a predominately Christian family and culture, so be it."

Buddhism

Buddhism is the fourth largest religion. The Dali Lama called Jesus a "fully enlightened being." But the Buddha declined to discuss the question I was trying to answer: Is there a God?[146]

Taoism

Taoism (pronounced "Dow-ism") didn't have anything to say about God either, so far as I could tell. Huston Smith said the original concept of *Tao* "was a concept too subtle to be grasped by the average mind."[147] I must have an average mind, for I had no idea what Taoism was about.

Confucianism

Confucius was a wise man who believed in one or more gods. But he spoke mainly about social ethics, not God.

Judaism

I read that Judaism doesn't seek converts, and I left it at that.[148]

Miscellaneous Religions

I read very little about religions that were mostly limited to remote places, races, or tribes. And I didn't consider any that required practices like never cutting your hair. I didn't decide there's no merit to any of those religions; I just didn't learn much about them.

I finally decided to follow the Hindu suggestion and start from where I was—in a predominantly Christian family and community. I was also impressed by the fact that the four largest religions revered Jesus. Moreover, they all share the Golden Rule that Jesus said summed up God's Law.

A Fresh Look

T. S. Eliot said that "at the end of all our exploring will be to arrive where we began and to know the place for the first time." That describes my experience with the religion of Christ.

A Bit of History

Written history is a condensed and oversimplified version of what happened. Otherwise it would take centuries longer to write history than it did for the events to occur. So my summary of early Christian history in the next few paragraphs will be extremely abbreviated. It will barely be enough to indicate how so many Christians have been extraordinarily charitable while others have been extremely cruel.

The expansion of Christianity in the first few centuries remains unmatched by any other movement that did not have political or military power. It became the most popular religion in the empire despite brutal efforts to suppress it. Christians fought back with nothing but the sword of their message, the shield of their faith, and the strength of their love. During a plague when others abandoned the sick at the first sign of symptoms, Christians remained to care for them. Christians became widely known for their kindness and courage.

The Emperor Constantine finally made it permissible to be a Christian. In fact, he became a Christian himself. The historian Will Durant summed up the results like this: "Caesar and Christ had met in the arena, and Christ had won."[149]

From a superb historical account, here is an interesting glimpse into something that took place under the rule of a subsequent emperor:

> The Emperor Julian . . . ordered his pagan priests to match Christian generosity because he instinctively knew what contemporary social scientists have since quantified: People are initially drawn to new religions not so much by doctrines as by the qualities they see in others already within the fold. Christian generosity played a crucial role . . . in the survival and growth of the early church.[150]

Tragically, a successor to Julian made it a crime to be anything other than a Christian. So Christendom had progressed from one extreme to the other, from being persecuted to being powerful. Some church officials proved they were not exceptions to the rule that power corrupts. They declared that anyone who did not accept certain doctrines was a "heretic." And they did to heretics what the Empire had once done to Christians; they had them tortured and killed. Of course those church officials were corrupted by their power, not by the religion of Jesus. In fact, they enforced their teachings *about* Jesus in ways that violated the teachings *of* Jesus.

Some atheists talk as if every church father was guilty of such cruelty. But many opposed it, such as John Chrysostom (347–407), who said, "God wishes all to be saved, but forces no one." And as shown in my first letter, other Christians introduced charity on a massive scale, started public hospitals, established universities, and fostered individual freedom, *including the freedom not to be a Christian*.[151] Yet some atheists persist in talking as if all Christians are alike, and always have been, even though they are currently divided into an estimated thirty-seven thousand denominations.[152]

Instead of trying to sort out all the doctrinal differences among Christians, I focused on the words of the one they all purported to follow. All the words attributed to Jesus in the four Gospels can be read in less than two hours, especially if you use one of those editions in which his words are printed in red.[153]

The "Jesus Seminar"

Before telling you how the words of Jesus affected me, I should comment on a group who called themselves "The Jesus Seminar." In 1985 they appointed themselves to decide if Jesus really said all the things attributed to him.

One of their members was a movie director. His résumé included *Showgirls*, *Robocop*, and *Basic Instinct*. That hardly qualified him as a Bible scholar, but it could explain how they got so much publicity.

Members of the Jesus Seminar voted individually on each passage with colored beads. Their founder explained the meanings of the colors like this:

- **Red**: Jesus said it or something very close to it.
- **Pink**: Jesus probably said something like it, although his words have suffered in transmission.
- **Gray**: Jesus did not say it, but the ideas are close to his own.
- **Black**: Jesus did not say it; the words represent the Christian community or a later point of view.[154]

They came up with a way to treat the resulting mix of colors with something they called "averages." Using that approach they more or less concluded that Jesus did not actually say some of the things attributed to him in the Gospels.

After reading some books by members of the Jesus Seminar I concluded that their so-called findings were subjective hunches based on personal biases. That was reinforced when I heard their cochair, John Dominick Crossan, speak at a university near my home. He spent most of his time talking about an experiment conducted by another professor. The experiment had nothing to do with Jesus. It concerned the explosion of the space shuttle *Challenger* in 1986. The day after the explosion a professor asked a class of freshman to write down how they first heard about it—who told them, where they were, etc.

He sealed their answers in an envelope. When they were seniors, the professor asked them to do the same thing. Not surprisingly, some of them didn't remember being asked the first time and some gave different answers.

From that "experiment" Crossan jumped to the conclusion that the Gospels are not reliable because they probably were not written down until several years after the events took place. Crossan failed to take into account one undisputed fact: the *Challenger* really did explode. The "experiment" he mentioned cast no doubt on that. It concerned the trivial question of how those students first heard about it, not whether the event took place. By contrast, many people at NASA *experienced* those events and later testified about them accurately and in detail. That professor's experiment was like asking the writers of the Gospels how they first heard someone mention a boy from Nazareth named Jesus, a common name back then. That was trivia compared to the dramatic events that followed in the years to come. Those who became his followers spent the rest of their lives telling their children, grandchildren, and converts about their *experiences* with him.

That experiment regarding the *Challenger* may have led to some interesting conversations over a few beers, but it didn't cast any doubt on the fact that the *Challenger* really did explode. And it certainly didn't support Crossan's inference that the events recorded in the Gospels didn't really happen.

Another fact Crossan failed to mention is that people were much better at memorization in New Testament times than we are today. They had no choice. They didn't have portable electronic devices that could hold megabytes of information. They didn't even have notepads or pencils. One page of papyrus cost a month's wages. And they couldn't carry an armload of scrolls everywhere they went. What we regard as phenomenal memories today were common back then. The time that elapsed before the Gospels were written down wasn't very long for that era—and their stories about Jesus were definitely not trivial.

I had the feeling Crossan was straining to justify a conclusion he had reached for some emotional reason, perhaps related to his leaving the priesthood. That feeling was reinforced by the way he became agitated by some perfectly reasonable questions from the audience.

One devastating critique of the Jesus Seminar has received high praise from both secular and religious scholars: *The Real Jesus: The Misguided Quest for the Historical Jesus and the Truth of the Traditional Gospels* by Luke Timothy Johnson, PhD. Dr. Johnson is the professor of New Testament and Christian origins in the Candler School of Theology at Emory University. His book politely but firmly smashes any semblance of credibility attributed to the Jesus Seminar.

My Tipping Point

Based on exhaustive research, Dr. Albert Schweitzer wrote the groundbreaking book *The Quest of the Historical Jesus* (which I think should have been translated *The Quest for the Historical Jesus*). It was published in 1906 and is still in publication today. The following lines from that book and from Dr. Schweitzer's autobiography, *Out of My Life and*

Thought, led me to take a break from reading *about* the Christian religion and focus on the words of its founder:

> There is deep significance in the fact that whenever we hear the sayings of Jesus we have to enter a realm of thought which is not ours.[155]

> The authentic sayings of Jesus are more or less self-evidencing. Coming in contact with one of them . . . you feel a thrill of recognition. They leap forth and take their proper place, where their vivid power becomes apparent.[156]

> There was a danger of our thrusting ourselves between men and the Gospels, and refusing to leave the individual man alone with the sayings of Jesus.[157]

That's what I did. I got alone with the sayings of Jesus. I wanted to see if they were "self-evidencing" as Schweitzer said. I picked up a modern translation of the New Testament in which his words were printed in red. I did my best to read them as if I had never seen them before.

All the words of Jesus in the four Gospels can be read in less time that it takes to watch a football game. Yet those few words have had a greater positive impact on more lives than all other words ever spoken, written, or enacted into law.

Reading his words proved to be my tipping point. Much of what Jesus said had a ring of truth. I was puzzled by some things he said, but he solved that problem by making two passages bench-marks for interpreting all the others—the Golden Rule and the dual commandments to love God with all we've got and to love others as much as we love ourselves. Those are the only two passages that Jesus said summed up

> All the words of Jesus in the four Gospels can be read in less time that it takes to watch a football game. Yet those few words have had a greater positive impact on more lives than all other words ever spoken, written, or enacted into law.

God's Law.[158] So I did not accept any interpretation of any other passage that was not consistent with those two.

I had returned, not to the roots of my earlier faith, but to the seeds of those roots—the words of Jesus. The Gospel according to Matthew reported that multitudes were amazed by the power of what he said.[159] So was I.

The Real Jesus

After reading the teachings *of* Jesus, I went back to focus on what the Gospels said *about* him. Instead of a stained-glass figure, I saw a real person. He got angry, sad, hungry, thirsty, tired, and sleepy.[160] He wept.[161] He often withdrew to be alone.[162] He once asked why God had forsaken him.[163] My impression was similar to that of Dr. Scott Peck, the psychiatrist who wrote the phenomenal best seller *The Road Less Traveled*. After writing that book Dr. Peck became a Christian and wrote *Further Along the Road Less Traveled*, in which he said: "I was absolutely thunderstruck by the extraordinary *reality* of the man I found in the Gospels. . . .

I discovered a man so incredibly real that no one could have made Him up."[164]

I, too, found the Gospel accounts to be credible and compelling. I've since read some scholarly works that reinforce that impression, including one by one of the world's most trusted historians, Will Durant (1885–1981). Toward the end of an in-depth analysis, he wrote:

> [N]o one reading these scenes can doubt the reality of the figure behind them. That a few simple men should in one generation have invented so powerful and appealing a personality, so lofty an ethic and so inspiring a vision of human brotherhood, would be a miracle far more incredible than any recorded in the Gospels.[165]

As a result of studying the words and life of Jesus I decided to try the experiment of following him. I would endeavor to obey the commands *of* Jesus without trying to sort out all the teachings *about* him. A Christian friend seemed to think it would have been enough just to adopt his beliefs about Jesus. That would have been easier. But Jesus warned that the right way isn't easy.[166] In any case, his original disciples chose to follow him before they were sure who he was. I figured I could do the same. And I found to be true something once said by Elton Trueblood, a Quaker theologian and former chaplain to both Harvard and Stanford universities: "This is a dangerous experiment, for it may change your life. . . . [Y]ou need not start with any preconceived judgment of who He is. Christ's first followers, as Schweitzer observed, were drawn to Him before they knew who He was. The same can happen to us today."[167]

I am pleased that my impressions of Jesus and the Gospels turned out to be consistent with those of such great scholars. But I still don't believe God requires us to become scholars to find the way. I have come to believe William Barclay was most likely right when he said, "In the last analysis, we can never argue a man into Christianity. All we can say is, 'Try it, and see.'"[168]

That is how I came to accept Jesus as who he said he was.

Of course this invites the question of whether those who never hear of Jesus are lost. I will discuss that in my next letter.

Sincerely,

John

Letter No.6

Regarding Doctrines

Dear Professor:

In August of 1987 a group of atheists gathered in my hometown to organize the Dallas chapter of American Atheists. The founder of the national organization, Madalyn Murray O'Hair, was there, but she stomped out when someone suggested atheists should be willing to shake hands with ministers.[169]

How would you feel, Professor, if I said Ms. O'Hair's behavior shows that all atheists are irrational? Well, that's how I feel when atheists recite strange beliefs and behaviors by a few Christians to disparage the entire religion. Sam Harris, for example, talks about one group's refusal to accept medical help, even for their children. Surely he knows they represent a miniscule percent of Christians.

I'll not waste your time talking about out-of-the-mainstream beliefs like that. But I will discuss a few beliefs that trouble many honest doubters. My willingness to talk about them may remind some readers of the old saying, "Fools rush in where angels fear to tread." They may

Having problems with certain beliefs is no reason to reject the Christian religion. Even the scholars who argue about them agree on that.

think I have no business tackling issues that Christian scholars have debated for centuries. But I will not presume to say which scholars are right. I just want to show why having problems with certain beliefs is no reason to reject the Christian religion. Even the scholars who argue about them agree on that.

I'll begin with a very unpleasant "doctrine" that atheists love to talk about.

Babies in Hell

Bishop Augustine of Hippo (354–430) said babies who die without having been baptized are going to hell. Someone later modified that to say such babies will spend eternity in a state of limbo outside of hell, but not in heaven. Of course many found that absurd and appalling. It's not the fault of a baby if it doesn't get baptized—and what a terrible thing to tell grieving parents. Moreover, it seems contrary to the way Jesus talked about little children: "Let the little children come to me, and do not hinder them, for the kingdom of heaven belongs to such as these."[170]

However, those old pronouncements about unbaptized babies are not valid reasons to reject the Christian religion. Pope Benedict XVI confirmed that neither one has ever been an official doctrine of the Church.

The Exclusivity Doctrine

There are an estimated 6,910 languages in the world. The Bible has only been translated into about 350 of those. Parts of the Bible are available in 2,212 languages, but that still leaves more than 4,000 without any portion of the Gospels.[171]

This highlights a question that has perplexed Christians for centuries: If the only way to heaven is to believe in Jesus, what is going to happen to people who never hear of him?

This came up in a debate I attended between the atheist Christopher Hitchens and three Christians. They were all very polite until someone mentioned the exclusivity doctrine. Hitchens took offense and said anyone who believes that doctrine it is a "wicked and delusional idiot."

The audience applauded.

I was not surprised. I've heard more hostile reactions to the exclusivity doctrine than any other belief associated with Christianity. It is often understood to mean that people who are never told about Jesus are going to hell. This presents the same problem as Augustine's old pronouncement about unbaptized babies. Just as it isn't the fault of a baby who doesn't get baptized, it's hardly a person's fault if they are never told about Jesus. For that matter, it's not their fault if they only hear about him from someone with no credibility or who doesn't tell the story right.

It's easy to see why the exclusivity doctrine troubles people, including many who believe it. It appears to mean billions will be punished for not believing something they never even heard. That offends our God-given sense of fairness. And it's hard to reconcile with the teachings of Jesus that say God is just and merciful.

Not being a theologian, I will not say no reasonable person can agree with the exclusivity doctrine. But I will say no one has to agree with it to be a Christian. Not even those who do agree with it say that. Moreover, most Christians do *not* agree with it. A major survey found that most Protestants—including majorities in each of the two largest conservative categories, evangelicals and Southern Baptists—believe "many religions can lead to eternal life."[172] And the catechism of the Catholic Church says: "Those who through no fault of their own do not know the Gospel of Christ or His Church, but who nevertheless seek God with a sincere heart, and, moved by grace, try in their actions to do His will as they know it through the dictates of their conscience—those too may achieve eternal salvation."[173]

The fact that a majority of Christians do not accept the exclusivity doctrine does raise an interesting question: How can a Bible-believing Christian *not* agree with it? According to one of the Gospels Jesus said, "No one comes to the Father except through me."[174] Another passage says, "Salvation is found in no one else."[175]

An answer that has been widely accepted came from the Jesuit theologian Karl Rahner (1904–1984). He agreed with the basic premise of the exclusivity doctrine—that following Jesus is the only way to salvation. However, he said a person can follow the *spiritual* Jesus without knowing about the *historical* Jesus. Many Bible passages are cited to support his view. Among them is one that says God's Law is written on every human heart and even pagans can show that law operating in their lives.[176] But what about those who *do* hear about the historical Jesus, but from people with no credibility, such as abusive parents? Or from good parents who say wrong things about him and teach their children to follow some other religion? Rahner said such people may reject the Christian religion as they understand it—or misunderstand it—but still follow the anonymous spirit of Christ in the context of another religion or apart from any religion. Some call that blasphemy. Others say it's blasphemous to say God lacks the power and love to reach and save such people.

Some Christians avoid the apparent unfairness of the exclusivity doctrine by saying people who don't accept Jesus in this life will have a chance to do so after he returns.

Dr. James Denison, a Baptist theologian, says everyone will have an opportunity to choose heaven even if the manner in which that will happen "has not been revealed to us."[177]

I will not offer an opinion on the merits of these views except to say they at least show why the exclusivity doctrine is not a reasonable basis for rejecting the Christian religion. Even those who accept it don't say you must agree with them to be a Christian. They might compare you to a person whose life can be saved only by a single drug, but who mistakenly believes there are other drugs that can do the job. That doesn't have to be a fatal mistake if the man will go ahead and take the life-saving drug anyway.[178]

That analogy to a life-saving drug reminds me of some advice a doctor friend once gave me. My son and I were preparing to go canoeing for a week in an Alaskan wilderness. The doctor recommended I take along some aspirin and chew them if I had symptoms of a heart attack. He said there are better drugs for treating heart attacks, but aspirin can be better than nothing and could save my life.

I wonder if something like that could be true of different religions. I believe in absolute truth, so I am not a relativist. But I can't believe any mere mortal has an exhaustive and exclusive knowledge of the truth. And I have come to believe that those who humbly seek a relationship with the source of all truth will be shown enough to live a life guided by the rule that Jesus said sums up God's Law and face eternity in peace. In other words, I have come to believe, as Jesus said, "He who seeks finds."[179]

In any event, it makes no sense to reject the Christian religion just because you don't accept a doctrine that most Christians don't accept either. In fact, you don't even have to form an opinion about it. First things first.

Hell and Fairness

When I was a child I heard hell described as a place of excruciating pain that will never end. Some years later it occurred to me that would eventually exceed any plausible measure of a fair punishment for more sins than anyone could possibly commit in a lifetime. And the notion that hell is a one-size-fits-all punishment for everyone didn't seem right either.

On the other hand, I found it easy to believe in ultimate justice for someone like Adolf Hitler, who created a hell on earth for millions. The idea that justice will eventually be done is imbedded in the human soul.

I eventually looked up "hell" in some Bible dictionaries

and was surprised by what I found. The English word "hell" is used for several words in the original languages, including *Gehenna, Hades,* and *Sheol.* Those words had different meanings, and their connotations changed from time to time. For example, Gehenna meant "Valley of Hinnon," a ravine south of Jerusalem. At different times it was used for sacrificing children by fire to a pagan idol, for burning the bodies of enemies, and then as a garbage dump that was usually burning. All those uses gave rise to the phrase "fires of hell." By New Testament times Gehenna had become a metaphor for the place where bad people go when they die. However, it was not universally thought to be a place of never-ending pain. A leading Bible dictionary says hell was regarded as "a final punishment, but not necessarily one that extends for all time."[180] Some scholars say the more extreme view of hell is actually a medieval concept from Dante's *Inferno,* the first part of the fourteenth-century epic poem *The Divine Comedy.*

Some Christian ministers from all across the fundamentalist-to-liberal spectrum have said there is no hell.[181] Not even for Adolf Hitler. I'm not prepared to bet my soul on that.

I reached two conclusions about hell: First, I can be a Christian without pretending to know anything about it. Second, I don't want to take the risk of finding out from personal experience.

Well, that's enough talk about unpleasant doctrines that trouble honest doubters. I could list more, but I hope the examples already discussed are enough to show why they are not valid excuses for rejecting the Christian religion. You don't even have to form an opinion about them. Even those who accept such doctrines agree on that—and not all Christians do accept them.

Now let's turn to a more uplifting doctrine that virtually all Christians do accept, notwithstanding some differences over details.

The Easter Story

No matter what you think about the resurrection of Jesus, the belief that it happened changed the world. And that belief is hard to explain if it didn't happen. Moreover, historians are in no position to say it didn't. This has been acknowledged by the agnostic scholar Bart D. Ehrman who said: "Historians, as historians, can't say exactly what happened with Jesus after his death, as to whether he was raised from the dead or not. What historians can say, though, *with some certainty* is that some of Jesus's followers came to believe that he'd been raised from the dead, and that, in fact, made all the difference in the world."[182]

After Jesus had been executed as a criminal, his followers did what you would expect—they withdrew in fear. Their hopes died with Jesus.

Then something happened that no one expected: his religion made a sudden comeback. Those who reject the resurrection have a problem. They don't have a good explanation for the resurgence of his followers who changed the world. Some endured torture and death rather than recant their eyewitness accounts. Many people may die for secondhand lies they believe are true, but not for firsthand lies they know are false.

Many people may die for secondhand lies they believe are true, but not for firsthand lies they know are false.

There are accounts of the resurrection in each of the four Gospels: Matthew, Mark, Luke, and John. It is also referred to in the book of Acts (a sequel to Luke) and in some of the New Testament letters of Paul. The notion that all those writers, separated by both time and distance, somehow collaborated to fabricate the story is more difficult to believe than the story itself.[183]

Some Christians are troubled because the New Testament accounts of the resurrection are not identical in every detail. But we lawyers tend to be suspicious of accounts by multiple witnesses that *are* exactly alike. That can raise suspicions that their stories were made up and memorized. The great historian Will Durant put this into perspective when he said that the differences "are of minutiae, not substance; in essentials the synoptic gospels agree remarkably well, and form a consistent portrait of Christ. . . . [and] they record many incidents that mere inventors would have concealed."[184]

The New Testament accounts just don't sound made-up. And they certainly don't sound like myths, which typically take a long time to develop. The great scholar J. B. Phillips said, "I have read, in Greek and in Latin, scores of myths, but I did not find the slightest flavor of myth here."[185]

Most arguments against the resurrection are examples

of a fallacy in logic called "reasoning in a circle." Stripped of their excess verbiage, they say, "The resurrection could not have happened because it could not have happened." Even when I was vacillating between agnosticism and atheism I saw no merit in an argument that begins by assuming its own conclusion. Besides, there have been medically confirmed cases where people have come back from clinical deaths. They're called "near" death experiences, but it would be more accurate to call them "temporary" death experiences.

At first I accepted the Easter story on faith as part of the experiment. But if you want to read an excellent account of historical evidence for the resurrection of Jesus, see Appendix B to the book *There Is a God* by the former atheist Antony Flew. That appendix was written by Bishop N. T. Wright, author of the definitive work *The Resurrection of the Son of God*. Bishop Wright's book runs over eight hundred pages, but his summary in the appendix to Flew's book is concise and convincing.

The Holy Bible

One of my favorite photographs is of the atheist Madalyn Murray O'Hair. It was taken by my friend Johnnie Godwin at the Russian International Book Fair in Moscow, Russia, in 1989. He and Ms. O'Hair both had booths there. Johnnie was giving away New Testaments in the Russian language. Ms. O'Hair was offering free literature promoting atheism.

Ms. O'Hair probably expected to be received enthusiastically because atheism had been the official policy in Russia since the 1920s. But she looks dejected in the photograph. Nobody is paying any attention to her even though the hall is jammed with people. Everyone else in the picture is headed toward Johnnie's booth. He and his colleagues gave away all ten thousand New Testaments they brought with them, and they took names and addresses so they could mail more to others later.

Meanwhile, no one took anything from Ms. O'Hair.

Through a translator, Johnnie asked one man why he wasn't interested in Ms. O'Hair's free literature. He said, "I have tried that. It did not work. I want a Bible."

Unbelief didn't work for me either. The faith experiment did. An important part of the experiment was to read from the Bible and let it speak for itself. Today my belief in the Bible is bolstered by the fact that many scientists accept it as true, including members of the American Scientific Affiliation: A Fellowship of Christians in Science.[186]

However, that doesn't explain why my belief in the Bible began to take root in the first place. I didn't know about the American Scientific Affiliation back then. I did know that many parts of the Bible had been corroborated by archaeological and historical research. That research has led many skeptics, including some former atheists, to believe the Bible.[187] That research is impressive. But it doesn't explain why the Bible became the world's most powerful book. The Bible had already become a powerful book before that research was done. In fact, that's *why* that research was done.

So something else must have been at work to give the Bible such power.

I believe the best way to understand why the Bible is so powerful is this: *just read it.* Herschel Hobbs, an elder statesman among Bible scholars, once said: "The Bible is its own best witness." One of my favorite examples of this comes from the book *Four Came Home* by Carroll Glines. It is about survivors of the famous World War II Tokyo raid led by Jimmy Doolittle. The four men featured in the book were captured and held prisoner for more than three years. They spent most of that time in solitary confinement and being tortured. Then someone slipped them a Bible they passed around. How the Bible affected them is only a small part of the book, but I don't see how anyone can read it and doubt that the Bible can save and profoundly change lives. You may scoff at that, but your skepticism will fade away if you read *Four Came Home*.

Mistakes in the Bible?

In 1631 the royal printers of the King James Version of the Bible mistakenly omitted the word "not" from the following commandment: "Thou shalt not commit adultery."[188] That edition came to be known as *The Sinners' Bible*. Charles I, the King of England, was so upset he made the printers appear before a Star Chamber and pay a fine.

The "corrected" King James Version of the Bible contains 773,746 words in sixty-six books. The Catholic version contains seven more books. And some books, like Psalms and Proverbs, are themselves collections of songs, poems, and aphorisms attributed to different people like David and Solomon. Those writings existed separately for many centuries before printing was invented and they were bound into a single volume. Yet many atheists (and some Christians) talk as if the Bible must be accepted or rejected on an all-or-none basis. They seem to think one tiny mistake would be like a dirty sock in a bowl of punch. But I can't see why every word in all those books must stand or fall together. If we applied that criterion to all other books, our libraries might be empty.

The writings in the Bible are based on copies made by hand over many centuries, so it's not surprising that some mistakes have been discovered. (Contrary to a popular misconception, many inerrantists acknowledge this but emphasize that the mistakes are in copies, not the originals.) The most significant mistake is the conclusion of Mark (chapter 16, verses 9–20). Many versions of the Bible published today note that passage is not in the earliest manuscripts. That comes as a relief to many Christians, as it attributes to Jesus these words: "In my name . . . they will pick up snakes with their hands; and when they drink deadly poison, it will not hurt them at all."

Many scholars say the other known mistakes are of little or no consequence.[189] They are like a few weeds in a field of wheat. It would make no sense to burn all that wheat just to get rid of the weeds.

When I started reading the Bible as part of my experiment I approached it like I panned for gold in Alaska: I looked for nuggets and didn't worry about the rest. Each time I read it, I found more nuggets of truth.

At first I didn't worry about whether the Bible was inspired. I just knew much of it was inspiring. That was reason enough to keep

> When I started reading the Bible as part of my experiment I approached it like I panned for gold in Alaska: I looked for nuggets and didn't worry about the rest.

reading it. And the more of the Bible I found to be deeply inspiring, the more of it I came to regard as divinely inspired.

I also found it helpful to consult Bible dictionaries and commentaries. For example, I assumed the references to "demons" just reflected a superstition of the times, until I read this:

> The ancient world believed unquestioningly and intensely in evil spirits. The air was so full of these spirits that it was not even possible to insert into it the point of a needle without coming against one. . . . They lived in unclean places. . . . One of their favorite ways of gaining an entry into a man's body was to lurk beside him while he ate, and to settle on his food."[190]

Does that sound familiar? Substitute "germs" for "spirits" and see how it sounds. The biblical demons were not ghostlike figures like those in horror movies. The ancient world thought evil spirits were invisible to the naked eye and settled on food. That was centuries before Louis Pasteur came up with the germ theory. So the old concept of demons turned out to be amazingly accurate.

I've also enjoyed reading books telling how the biblical writings were chosen. A good short account is *Introducing the Bible* by William Barclay, which does an outstanding job of putting copying mistakes into perspective. An excellent and more detailed account is *An Introduction to the Bible*, coauthored by Clyde E. Fant,

Donald W. Musser, and Mitchell G. Reddish.

However, reading about the Bible without reading the Bible itself is like reading about a symphony and not listening to the music.

A Late Letter from My Father

When I was six years old my dad volunteered to join the army during World War II. He was thirty-six. While in officer's training at Camp Claiborne in Louisiana, he wrote me several letters. But the night before he shipped out to go overseas he wrote one that was very special.

Forty-five years would pass before I saw that letter. By then I was fifty-one. I found it while helping my mother move. She had hidden it from me when I was a child because it hinted that Dad might not survive the war. He did survive and returned home to a great life. But he died several years before I discovered that letter. I'm glad I was alone when I found it so nobody could see me weeping.

I never doubted Dad loved me, but I don't recall that he ever said so before he wrote that letter. In the letter he made it clear that he loved me more than his own life and that if he had to die in the war so I could live in freedom, he would be glad to pay that price.

Dad had his faults but was a terrific father. He took me fishing and hunting a lot. We took vacations in the mountains of Colorado. We canoed and camped in Texas for days at a time on the Brazos River and on beautiful lakes. After the war he became a scoutmaster and treated me as if I was a member of his troop even though I wasn't old enough. When racial discrimination was still the norm

> I will not argue with anyone who is skeptical about the Bible. I just urge them to do what I did. *Read it.*

in the South where we lived, Dad explained to me why it was wrong. And he gave me other moral advice that served me well the rest of my life.

I have often felt inadequate, but never more than right now as I write this. I am groping for words to express the depth of gratitude I feel for Dad. Words fail me, but I am absolutely certain of this: *my gratitude for Dad and the love he expressed in that letter are not accidental results of random collisions of subatomic particles in an unplanned, godless universe.*

Reading the Bible takes me back to that letter. Parts of the Bible are like letters from my heavenly Father. God is saying to me despite all my failings, "I am very fond of you, and everything is going to be all right."

I will not argue with anyone who is skeptical about the Bible. I just urge them to do what I did. *Read it.* I trust it will speak for itself as it has throughout the ages.

To sum up my experience with the Bible I will borrow these words from the autobiography of Helen Keller, who had to read it in braille:

> I began to read the Bible long before I could understand it. Now it seems strange to me that there could have been a time when my spirit was deaf to its wondrous harmonies. . . .
>
> But how shall I speak of the glories I have since discovered in the Bible? I have read it with

an ever-broadening sense of joy and inspiration;
and I love it as I love no other book.[191]

Other Doctrinal Questions

When confronted with other doctrinal issues I often think of a pivotal moment in the life of Dr. Albert Schweitzer. While in medical school he began raising money to establish a hospital in an African jungle. Finally, as he wrote in his autobiography, "When I was certain that I could collect funds enough for the establishment of a small hospital, I made a definite offer to the Paris Missionary Society to go at my own expense to serve its mission field on the River Ogowé from the centrally situated station at Lambaréné."[192]

Schweitzer faced one last hurdle: a committee had to approve his proposal. Some of the "strictly orthodox" members wanted to examine his beliefs. So they summoned Schweitzer to appear before them to answer questions.

Schweitzer refused. They had rejected a candidate for another position, not because he held an unorthodox view, but because he had no opinion on a certain matter. Schweitzer felt the matter was not that important, so he sent word that he would only answer one question—the one Jesus put to his disciples: "Will you follow me?" Schweitzer said he had already given an unconditional yes to that one. He felt that answer, combined with his medical qualifications and his willingness to pay his own way, should be enough if they really wanted to reduce suffering.[193]

Following a heated debate, a slim majority finally accepted Schweitzer's proposal, but with a precondition.

He had to agree not to preach views that might trouble other missionaries. He agreed, as he wanted to alleviate human suffering more than he wanted to teach theology to the natives.

Schweitzer became as famous in his day as Mother Teresa was in hers. He was awarded the Nobel Prize for Peace in 1952. To avoid being away from his hospital, Schweitzer asked a friend to accept the prize for him and the money that came with it. He used the money to build a facility for leprosy patients near his hospital. He was still serving there when he died at the age of ninety in 1965.

Inspired by Dr. Schweitzer's example, I came up with a personal test for deciding what to do when confronted with a doctrinal issue. I spend no time on it unless I can imagine myself praying about it like this:

> Lord, I'm going to spend time and energy studying this issue because that's more important than using that time and energy to volunteer at that wonderful place that helps people who are blind. They will just have to wait while I occupy myself with this interesting question. And when the end comes, oh Lord, please judge me as if I had helped the blind instead of doing what I am about to do. Amen.

Of course that prayer is satire. I never really say it. But keeping it in mind helps me keep my priorities straight. For example, a friend once asked what I thought about the doctrine of predestination. At the risk of offending him I said, "I'm not going to worry about that until the last starving child has been fed." He smiled and said he felt the same way.

Not all doctrinal issues can be avoided that easily. Some concern personal choices regarding sex, abortion, gambling, and the use of alcohol and other drugs. But I'll not share my views on those here as people can disagree with me and still engage in the faith experiment.

I was tempted to end this letter with a long list of doctrinal questions I have decided not to answer, but I didn't want to leave the impression that no one else should deal with them. Some people—such as seminary professors and members of the clergy—need to study many of those questions. But it would be a poor use of my time to learn as much as they know about religion, just as it would be a waste of their time to learn as much as I know about law. The most important question we all need to answer is one asked by Jesus and answered by Dr. Schweitzer: "Will you follow me?" I finally said yes, and that made all the difference.

Now, Professor, you may be glad to hear that my next letter will be my last. And it won't be long. But it could be the most important one.

Sincerely,

John

Letter No. 7

Regarding Purpose

Dear Professor:

I begin this final letter with two questions I ask students to think about in my college course on leadership: What is your main mission in life? To the extent you succeed in that mission, will that make the world a better place? Some students have told me that second question caused them to reconsider their answer to the first one.

You have clearly stated your mission in life, Professor, and you've said, "I do everything in my power" to achieve it.[194] It relates to a choice you've made about God that you express as follows: "I cannot know for certain but I think God is very improbable, and I live my life on the assumption that he is not there."[195] So your declared mission is to persuade as many people as you can to make that same choice—to live their lives on the "assumption" that God does not exist—even though you cannot prove that assumption is correct.

You have certainly made progress toward that goal with your book *The God Delusion*. Other books defending atheism mainly appeal to readers who already agree with the authors. But while reading your book I had a feeling it was different. Although I believe your arguments are flawed (for reasons respectfully pointed out in my previous letters), your style of writing can be persuasive. You have won more than a few over to atheism. That is evident from testimonials on your website.

So let's move on to the second question: Is your success making the world a better place?

Converts and Consequences

If your converts had been noxious extremists, their abandonment of religion would be an improvement. But as you've acknowledged, Professor, religious extremists won't even open a book like yours.[196] So you are not doing anything to reduce the kind of religion you call harmful.

Instead, you expressly target "moderates" who are *not* extremists, especially those who "need only a little encouragement" to give up their religion.[197] And you have persuaded many of them to abandon the path of faith.

You don't seem to realize how tragic that is. That path could have led many of them to support humanitarian charities. This is not speculation. It is supported by studies based on massive data referred to in my first letter. Those studies found that even people of *moderate* faith donate a lot more money and volunteer more hours to charities than secularists. They give more to secular charities than secularists. They also give more blood.

Due to the absence of humanitarian actions at least some of your converts would have taken, people somewhere may be waiting on food, medical help, and other aid that will never come. Perhaps some have already lived in misery and died in agony as a result of your "success."

I am not being overly dramatic. Each time you persuade someone to give up their religion you remove them from the pool of people most likely to support charities and to donate blood. And you can't say that will be offset by a reduction in suffering caused by religious extremists—you have admitted religious extremists won't read your book.[198]

You denounce extremists because they cause human suffering. But aren't you also perpetuating human suffering, albeit with different motives? That leads to another question: What *are* your motives?

Please don't insult us with that old line that you must speak the truth regardless of the consequences. You've admitted you're not certain your position *is* the truth. You've acknowledged the obvious truth that you can't prove there is no God. Atheism, to use your own word, is an "assumption" you can't be certain is correct.[199]

Why, then, are you trying so hard to persuade people to assume something you can't prove? You cannot prove believers are wrong, yet you want them just to *assume* you are right. You're urging them to bet their souls on your unproven guess. Common sense says that's the dangerous side of the bet. The other side has everything to gain and nothing to lose, both in this life and the next.

I have friends who have lost children to death. Their grief is lessened by the hope of being reunited with them someday. You can't prove that won't happen, yet you've made it your life's work to crush their hopes. You don't seem to care about their feelings. *In that respect, aren't you like the religious extremists you condemn for having no regard for the feelings of others?*

I'll ask it again: What are your motives?

Of course I can't be sure of your motives because I can't read your mind. But do you have the courage to get alone in a room and give gut-level, honest answers to the following questions?

- Have I let my anger toward evil religion boil over into a prejudice against all religion?
- In my book *The God Delusion*, why am I silent about the religious people who provide humanitarian aid to billions around the world?
- Am I allowing my ego or false pride to prevent me from admitting I've been wrong all these years?
- Am I concerned about losing income from my books promoting atheism?
- Do I crave the attention and notoriety I get by being an outspoken atheist?

The Perfect Motive

I have studied a lot about motives. As a trial lawyer I sometimes had to introduce evidence of motives in court. Later, as a business attorney, I had to figure out hidden motives while negotiating contracts. I've done that with some success in different cultures around the world. My college courses in psychology and sociology proved to be helpful in those situations.

The most profound work on motives I've read is a small volume called *Man's Search for Meaning* by Viktor Frankl, MD, PhD. He was a Holocaust survivor. Almost fifty years after his book was published it was still one of the "ten most influential books" according to a survey by the Library of Congress (the Bible was No. 1).

Prior to the war Dr. Frankl was the head of psychiatry at Vienna's Rothschild Hospital. That is where he began to develop his theory about motives. His new approach to psychotherapy was even effective with people who were suicidal. He treated thousands of them with phenomenal success.

Dr. Frankl's studies were interrupted in 1942 when the Nazis took him to a concentration camp. They murdered his pregnant wife, Tilley, in the gas "showers." They killed his parents and brothers. He was the victim of horrible treatment, but he survived. His observations in the camp reinforced his theory about motives.

After being liberated by American soldiers near the end of World War II, Dr. Frankl dictated *Man's Search for Meaning* in just nine days. Yet, according to *The American Journal of Psychiatry*, he contributed "perhaps the most significant thinking since Freud and Adler."[200] Freud had theorized that man's greatest desire is for pleasure. Adler said it's for power. Frankl believed man's greatest desire is not for pleasure or power, but for *purpose*.[201]

Dr. Frankl's findings may help explain the extraordinary popularity of the book *The Purpose Driven Life* by Rick Warren. We all want our lives to count for something.

Dr. Frankl called his approach "logotherapy," from the Greek word for "meaning."[202] He said:

- "Man's search for meaning is the primary motivation in his life and not a 'secondary rationalization' of instinctual drives."[203]
- "Man's main concern is not to gain pleasure or to avoid pain but rather to see a meaning in his life."[204]
- "What a person actually needs is not a tensionless state but rather the striving and struggling for a worthwhile goal."[205]

A key word in that last statement is "worthwhile."

Reflecting on forty years of practicing law has convinced me Dr. Frankl was right. I saw some clients strive for their own happiness without much regard for the needs of others. Some acquired great wealth but were negative and miserable. Others used their wealth to help others and were positive and upbeat. Each of us has a core desire to live for a worthwhile purpose—and nothing is more worthwhile than helping others in need.

Frankl's "Postscript"

Forty years after the original publication of *Man's Search for Meaning*, Dr. Frankl added a "Postscript" to a new edition. It tells about an experiment he conducted before the war during the Great Depression. The experiment involved patients suffering from "unemployment neurosis." They equated being jobless with being useless and felt their lives had no meaning. Frankl persuaded them to "fill their abundant though unwanted free time with some sort of unpaid but meaningful activity." They did a lot of volunteer work, and "their depression disappeared although their economic situation had not changed and their hunger was the same."[206]

Frankl found that an effective way to help others is to persuade *them* to help others. Many studies have confirmed his findings.[207]

Rich or poor, well or ill, those who engage in worldly charity occupy the top of the happiness pyramid.[208] I'm not talking about the kind of happiness that makes us laugh out loud, although Frankl acknowledged that can be good for us, too. I'm speaking of the more enduring satisfaction of knowing we've been of service to others in need. That is our deepest desire and highest calling.

You, Professor, are urging people to give up the most effective motive there is for being charitable—religious faith. *Can't you see how that hurts not only those who need to receive help, but those who need to give it?*

This brings us back to the question of your motives.

As I said, I can't read your mind. But I have read your book. I've listened to your conversation with Ben Stein in the documentary movie *Expelled.* I've seen you on television and your website. I've seen the newspaper stories with a picture of you standing beside a London bus adorned with colorful balloons and a banner saying, "There's Probably No God." You were grinning with childlike pride.[209]

At least one of your motives seems pretty obvious to me. You share it with those "shiny-suit-ed bouffant-haired tele-va-ngelists" you belittle

> Can't you see how that hurts not only those who need to receive help, but those who need to give it?

in your book. You really enjoy your notoriety. But isn't a terrible price being paid for whatever pleasure you get from all that attention?

Your Life's Purpose

I hope you will someday use your notoriety for a worthwhile purpose, Professor. The former atheist Antony Flew finally did. If he had not been widely regarded as the leading atheist, his belief in God would not have made worldwide headlines. Even though he never became religious (so far as I know) his book *There Is a God* certainly knocked down a barrier to religious faith for others. And he said the religion of Jesus is "the one to beat" and he was "entirely open" to becoming a Christian.[210]

You, Professor, could have a greater impact than Professor Flew. His writings as an atheist mainly appealed to intellectuals. You have found a larger audience. So you will likely receive even more public notice if you change your mind. Imagine all the good you could do if you tried the experiment and became a person of faith. You could write a book about that. I'll bet it would be a runaway best seller. Just think of how many malnourished and starving children could be fed with proceeds from that book. Think of those who could be clothed, sheltered, healed, educated, and helped in so many other ways. (Before you ask, yes, I intend to use my profits from this book for worldly charity.)

You have boasted about something that gives me hope, Professor. You have said that you, unlike many of your religious critics, are willing to change your mind.[211] If you really meant that and were not just saying it for effect, you must be ready to try what may be the only thing that *can* change your mind—a personal experiment in faith.

You can start right now by praying privately. Remember what my friend told me: "Answers to my prayers will never convince you there is a God. Only answers to your own prayers will do that. And you will never have any answered if you don't pray." No one else has to know you're praying, unless of course there is a God who hears you. Even then your prayers can remain a private matter between you and God. In the Sermon on the Mount, Jesus said that is what prayer is supposed to be.

Another essential step is to engage in worldly charity. You're going to be doing something the rest of your life, so it might as well be something worthwhile. It is clearly more worthwhile to feed the hungry than to persuade others to abandon the faith that motivates them to feed the hungry. It is obviously more worthwhile to assist the blind than to say people should not believe in a God they can't see. And it is certainly more worthwhile to support faith-based organizations that provide humanitarian aid to *billions* than to attack the religious reasons for all the good they do.

In short, Professor, the remainder of your life can be worthwhile if you will stop spending so much time and effort making arguments against God that you admit are not conclusive, and start using that time and energy to help others who desperately need food, water, clothes, shelter, healing, and other forms of humanitarian assistance. If you don't, you run the risk of someday having to look back at your life from the dark valley of deep regrets.

I pray you will choose to proceed with the faith experiment and discover, as I have, that a person with an experience is never at the mercy of someone who only has an argument.

God's peace,

Acknowledgments

My deepest gratitude to:

Milli Brown, publisher and CEO of Brown Books Publishing Group, who exemplifies the best qualities I tried to teach in my university course on leadership. Her door is always open to her authors, notwithstanding other massive demands on her time. And to her "dream team," who patiently guided me and my book through the publishing process: **Auburn Layman**, editorial coordinator; **David Leach**, director of publishing; **Jessica Burnham,** production manager; **Omar Mediano**, art director; **Cathy Williams**, national marketing director; **Cindy Birne**, public relations director; and **Rayven Williams**, project coordinator.

Clyde Fant, who became my pastor and then my friend many years ago during a pivotal stage of my faith experiment. Some things he said planted the seed that grew into this book.

Johnnie Godwin, a lifelong friend. Without his personal encouragement and professional advice, I might never have finished the first draft.

Foy Valentine, a world-class scholar who motivated me to complete the manuscript and then asked his friend **Millard Fuller** to read and endorse it.

Kathleen Davis Niendorff, a brilliant publishing consultant and literary agent in Austin, Texas, who gave me encouragement and wise counsel when I needed both.

Rebecca Dark, an English professor at Dallas Baptist University, who is a genius at suggesting small changes that add up to huge improvements.

The kids at Camp John Marc—Special Camps for Special Kids who taught me by their example that I have no right complain about anything and that I have every reason to share my profits from this book with others who need them more than I do.

Endnotes

1. Antony Flew, *There Is a God: How the World's Most Notorious Atheist Changed His Mind* (New York: HarperOne, 2007),112. Antony Flew made worldwide headlines when he publicly disclosed his belief in God in 2004 while speaking at New York University. He had privately begun to reject atheism some twenty years earlier. He gave an account of his journey in *There Is a God*, in which he cites "compelling and irrefutable" evidence of God (112) for which God is "the only viable explanation" (121). He also says the only satisfactory explanation for certain facts about DNA is "an infinitely intelligent Mind" (132). His book mainly focuses on scientific proof of God, not on a personal relationship with God. When he wrote the book he was still pondering the question: "Where do I go from here?" He said the religion of Jesus is "the one to beat" and he was "entirely open" to becoming a Christian (156–157). At his request a Christian scholar wrote an appendix to his book that makes a compelling case for Christianity.

2. Christopher Hitchens, *God Is Not Great* (New York: Twelve, 2007), 280.

3. Sam Harris, *The End of Faith* (New York: W. W. Norton, 2005), 214.

4. Ibid., 301, n 24. Harris wrote a second book, *Letter to a Christian Nation* (New York: Knopf, 2006), but its stated purpose is not to debate the existence of God. It is "to arm secularists in our society, who believe that religion should be kept out of public policy, against their opponents on the Christian Right" (viii). Even some atheists don't agree with that objective as it could erode freedom of speech, a right cherished by both atheists and believers. Moreover, Harris's second book is riddled with factual misstatements pointed out by Michael Patrick Leahy in *Letter to an Atheist* (Nashville: Harperth River Press, 2007).

5. All references to Dawins's book, except where otherwise indicated, come from the original hardback edition of *The God Delusion* (New York: Houghton Mifflin, 2006). Due to the addition of a preface within the paperback edition (New York: A

Mariner Book, Houghton Mifflin, 2008), the page numbers are not the same in both editions. Therefore, for the convenience of readers using the paperback edition, all citations for *The God Delusion* will include parenthetical references to the page numbers in the later paperback edition.

6. Jim Holt, "Beyond Belief," *New York Times*, October 22, 2006, http://www.nytimes.com/2006/10/22/books/review/Holt.t.html?_r=1&pagewanted=1&or.

7. Two books by former atheists which make strong cases that DNA and RNA prove the existence of an Intelligent Creator are: Antony Flew, *There Is a God*, 74–81, 123–132, and Francis S. Collins, *The Language of God: A Scientist Presents Evidence for Belief* (New York: Free Press, 2006), 1–7, 109–142. *See also* John C. Lennox, *God's Undertaker: Has Science Buried God?* (Oxford: Lion, 2007), 127–138.

8. Richard Dawkins, *The God Delusion*, 1 (paperback, 23).

9. Dinesh D'Souza, *What's So Great About Christianity?* (Washington, DC: Regnery, 2007), 213–221. D'Souza includes another ten million victims of Hitler and makes a strong case that Hitler was an atheist. I did not include Hitler's victims in the count because I am not aware of any proof that Hitler ever declared himself to be atheist even though he surrounded himself with people who did.

10. A vast majority of killings attributed to religious extremists are from the Crusades. Some historians say those should not be counted as acts of religious extremists because the Crusades were waged for political and territorial reasons when the Church was a tool of the state. Likewise, the Spanish Inquisition was carried out at the behest of rulers in Spain and notwithstanding efforts by the pope and the Church to stop it. To avoid debating those issues I have counted both as acts of religious extremists. No one knows how many died in the Crusades but the guesses range from less than one million to eight million if you include those who died from ordinary illnesses and injuries while traveling. I have used the upper end of those guesses even though they are almost certainly exaggerated. Historians estimate that the Inquisitions resulted in 1,500–4,000 deaths over 350 years. Estimates for executions of "witches" in Europe may have been as high as 100,000. The number said to have

been sentenced to death in the Salem witch trials ranges from 19–128. If you add up all these maximum estimates and add everyone killed by Islamic terrorists and because of hostilities between other religious groups, the total can be pushed almost as high as ten million. (As noted earlier, over 80 percent of that figure consists of guesses at how many died during the Crusades, using a figure that is almost certainly exaggerated.) The "maximized" total still adds up to less than 10 percent of all those killed by atheistic regimes. For an analysis of historical data on these figures see Dinesh D'Souza, *What's So Great About Christianity?*, 203–211. *See also* Bruce Sheiman, *An Atheist Defends Religion: Why Humanity Is Better Off With Religion than Without It* (New York: Alpha, 2009), xi, 117–141.

11. Bruce Sheiman, *An Atheist Defends Religion*, xi, 117–141. *See also* Dinesh D'Souza, *What's So Great About Christianity?*, 203–211.

12. Matthew 23:13–36; 21:13; Mark 11:17; Luke 19:46.

13. Simon LeVay, *When Science Goes Wrong: Twelve Tales from the Dark Side of Discovery* (New York: A Plume Book, 2008), vii.

14. Robert A. Watson and Ben Brown, *"The Most Effective Organization in the U. S." Leadership Secrets of The Salvation Army* (New York: Crown Business, 2001). As quoted on the cover.

15. Richard Dawkins, *The God Delusion*, 306 (paperback, 346).

16. In Matthew 7:12, Jesus said the Golden Rule sums up God's Law.

17. Richard Dawkins, *The God Delusion*, 5–6 (paperback, 28).

18. For a brief account of the Galileo case, see Dinesh D'Souza, *What's So Great About Christianity?*, 101–111. *See also* John C. Lennox, *God's Undertaker*, 22–25.

19. Richard Dawkins, *The God Delusion*, 278 (paperback, 315).

20. Ibid., 273 (paperback, 309).

21. Ibid., 278 (emphasis added) (paperback, 316).

22. Ibid., 278 (paperback, 315–316).

23. Ibid., 278 (paperback, 316).

24. Arthur C. Brooks, *Who Really Cares: America's Charity Divide* (New York: Basic Books, 2006).

25. Ibid., xi.

26. Most of the advertising and other publicity about the book *Who Really Cares* emphasized that political conservatives give more of their own money than liberals, which came as a surprise to the author and much of the public. However, chapter 2 of the book, "Faith and Charity," makes it clear that liberals who are religious give almost as much as conservatives who are religious. The correlation of charity to political views just reflects the fact that there are more religious people among conservatives than among liberals. The most common denominator of personal and voluntary giving on both sides is religious faith. So religion trumps politics when it comes to charity.

27. Richard Dawkins, *The God Delusion*, 226 (paperback, 258).

28. In Matthew 7:12, Jesus said the Golden Rule sums up God's Law. Romans 2:13–15 says God's Law in written on all human hearts, including those of pagans who do not have the written scriptures containing the Law.

29. Arthur C. Brooks, *Who Really Cares*, 34.

30. A very short book on happiness based on huge volumes of research is *The Happiness Equation: 100 Factors That Can Add To or Subtract From Your Happiness* by Bridget Grenville-Cleave, Ilona Boniwell, and Tina Tessina (Avon, MA: Adams Media, 2008). It is divided into brief "entries" instead of chapters. To see the connection between faith, charity, and happiness, see entries 70 (p. 99), 94 (p. 127), and 96 (p. 129). *See also* Allen Luks with Peggy Payne, *The Healing Power of Doing Good: The Health and Spiritual Benefits of Helping Others* (New York: Fawcett Columbine, 1991); Arthur C. Brooks, *Who Really Cares*, 137–160; Bruce Sheiman, *An Atheist Defends Religion*.

31. Frank I. Luntz, *What Americans Really Want . . . Really: The Truth about Our Hopes, Dreams, and Fears* (New York: Hyperion, 2009), 161.

32. Vincent Carroll and David Shiflett, *Christianity on Trial: Arguments Against Anti-Religious Bigotry* (San Francisco: Encounter Books, 2002).

33. Ibid., 52.

34. "Quran" was more commonly spelled "Koran" for many decades.

Today it is sometimes spelled with an apostrophe after the *r*, as in "Qur'an." I have not found an English spelling that does not offend at least a few Muslims for reasons I have never understood. To minimize this problem I've chosen a spelling that appears to be most widely used as of this writing. In any event, the Quran explicitly prohibits suicide. It also forbids "compulsion in matters of religion." The Hadith (sayings of Muhammad) requires Muslims to treat Jews and Christians with affection. Muhammad said, "God will not be merciful to those who are not merciful to others," and he taught a version of the Golden Rule, which will be discussed in another letter.

35. Bruce Sheiman, *An Atheist Defends Religion,* 128. *See also* Marc Sageman, *Leaderless Jihad* (Philadelphia: University of Pennsylvania Press, 2008).

36. Louise Richardson, *What Terrorists Want: Understanding the Enemy, Containing the Threat* (New York: Random House, 2006), 61.

37. Ibid.

38. Timothy George, "Is Christ Divided?," *Christianity Today,* July 2005, 31. *See also* "denominationalism" in the most current *Oxford World Encyclopedia.*

39. "Eco-activists plead guilty in firebombings," *Los Angeles Times,* November 10, 2006.

40. Richard Dawkins, "Preface to the Paperback Edition," *The God Delusion* (New York: A Mariner Book, Houghton Mifflin Company, 2008), 15.

41. Ibid.

42. Richard Dawkins, *The God Delusion,* 5–6 (paperback, 28).

43. Richard Dawkins, "Preface to the Paperback Edition," *The God Delusion,* 17–18.

44. Bruce Sheiman, *An Atheist Defends Religion,* vii, xiii.

45. Ibid., 73.

46. Ibid., xv.

47. Andy Simmons, "Tragedy Tomorrow, Comedy Tonight," *Reader's Digest,* September 2008, 112.

48. J. Edwin Orr, *The Faith that Persuades* (New York: Harper & Row, 1977), 19. Bertrand Russell called himself an agnostic in a debate because he couldn't prove that God does not exist.

49. Richard Dawkins, *The God Delusion*, 51 (paperback, 73–74).

50. Ibid., 158 (paperback, 189).

51. Dawkins conceded this same point in *The God Delusion*, 50–51 (paperback, 73–74).

52. Richard Dawkins, *The God Delusion*, 52–53 (paperback, 76). The statement following the colon is a short summary of thoughts expressed by Dawkins, not a direct quote.

53. Ibid., 82n (paperback, 106n).

54. Antony Flew, *There Is a God*, 112, 121, 132.

55. Ibid., 56, 89, 135.

56. Michael Guillen, PhD, is an Emmy award–winning physicist who taught at Harvard and became a science correspondent for ABC News. Dr. Guillen is one of the most refreshing personalities I've seen on TV. In addition to books on science, he's written about his faith in *Can a Smart Person Believe in God?* (Nashville: Nelson Books, 2004). His enthusiastic answer is "Yes!" His book refers to other highly respected scientists who believe in God.
Francis S. Collins, MD, PhD, was the director of the National Human Genome Institute, which has achieved one of the most significant scientific breakthroughs in history: mapping the human DNA. In his book *The Language of God* (New York: Free Press, 2006), Dr. Collins shares his own journey from atheism to faith and explains there is no real conflict between scientific facts and religious truth.
John Polkinghorne was a knighted professor of mathematical physics at Cambridge who became an Anglican priest. He is known internationally both as a theoretical physicist and as a theologian. He has written several books, including *Belief in God in an Age of Science* (New Haven, CT: Yale University Press, 1998).
Russell Stannard is a distinguished nuclear physicist who headed the physics department at a university in London. He has authored several best-selling books on science and religion, including *The God Experiment: Can Science Prove the Existence of*

God? (New Jersey: HiddenSpring, 1999).
Dr. Timothy Johnson, MD, MPH, is the medical editor for
ABC News. He also holds joint positions in medicine at
Harvard University and Massachusetts General Hospital in
Boston. He is the founding editor of the *Harvard Medical
School Health Letter* and coeditor of another Harvard medical
publication. He gives an account of his personal faith in *Finding
God in the Questions* (Dowers Grove, IL: InterVarsity Press,
2004).

57. Sharon Begley, "Science Finds God," *Newsweek*, July 20, 1998,
46–52. *See also* Robert Wright, "Science, God and Man," *Time*,
December 28, 1992, 38–44.

58. http://www.asa3.org.

59. Richard Dawkins, *The God Delusion*, 71–72 (paperback, 97).

60. John Marks Templeton and Kenneth Seeman Giniger, ed.,
Spiritual Evolution (Philadelphia: Templeton Foundation Press,
1998).

61. Alister and Joanna Collicutt McGrath, *The Dawkins Delusion?*
(Dowers Grove, IL: InterVarsity Press, 2007), 42–44; John
C. Lennox, *God's Undertaker: Has Science Buried God?*, 16–17;
Timothy Keller, *The Reason for God* (New York: Dutton, 2008),
89. The original survey was done by psychologist James Leuba.

62. "Science and Belief," The Pew Forum on Religion & Public
Life, based on a poll taken in 2009, http://pewforum.org/
science-and-Bioethics/Scientists-and-Belief.aspx?.

63. Michael Dowd, *Thank God for Evolution: How the Marriage of
Science and Religion Will Transform Your Life and Our World*, rev.
2nd ed. (New York: Viking/Penguin, 2008).

64. Francis S. Collins, *The Language of God: A Scientist Presents
Evidence for Belief* (New York: Free Press, 2006).

65. Psalm 90:4. *See also* 2 Peter 3:8.

66. Sam Harris, *Letter to a Christian Nation*, x.

67. Michael Patrick Leahy, *Letter to an Atheist*, 4–16.

68. Simon LeVay, *When Science Goes Wrong: Twelve Tales from the
Dark Side of Discovery*, vii.

69. David Freedman, *Wrong: Why Experts Keep Failing Us* (New York: Little Brown, 2010). This list of the types of experts who mislead us is quoted from a footnote to the word "Experts" in the subtitle of the book.

70. Richard Dawkins, *The God Delusion*, 51 (paperback, 74).

71. Ibid.

72. Sam Harris, *The End of Faith*, 226.

73. Blaise Pascal, *Pensées and Other Writings* (New York: Oxford University Press, 2008), 154.

74. Abu Hamed al-Ghazali, *The Alchemy of Happiness* (New York: Sharpe Publishers, 1991), 42–43.

75. Richard Dawkins, *The God Delusion*, 103–105 (paperback, 130–132).

76. Pascal, *Pensées*, 153.

77. Kevin Miller and Ben Stein, *Expelled: No Intelligence Allowed*, directed by Nathan Frankowski (Premise Media Corporation, 2008).

78. Richard Dawkins, *The God Delusion*, 50–51 (paperback, 73–74).

79. Ibid., 50 (paperback, 73).

80. Ibid., 316 (paperback, 355).

81. Christopher Hitchens, *God Is Not Great*, 214.

82. Richard Dawkins, *The God Delusion*, 104 (paperback, 131).

83. Pascal, *Pensées*, 156.

84. Richard Dawkins, *The God Delusion*, 103–105 (paperback, 130).

85. William James, *The Will to Believe* (New York: Image Books Doubleday, 1995), 33.

86. Templeton, *Spiritual Evolution*. This is a collection of ten essays by scientists. *See also* Francis S. Collins, MD, PhD, *The Language of God*. Francis S. Collins is the former director of the National Human Genome Institute, which achieved one of the most significant scientific breakthroughs in history: mapping the human DNA.

87. Richard Dawkins, *The God Delusion*, 308 (paperback, 347).

88. Sam Shoemaker, *Extraordinary Living for Ordinary Men* (Grand Rapids, MI: Zondervan Publishing House, 1965), 28.

89. Richard Dawkins, *The God Delusion,* 87–92 (paperback, 112–117).

90. Carl Gustav Jung, MD, *Psychology & Religion* (New Haven, CT: Yale University Press, 1938), 113–114.

91. Antony Flew, *There Is a God,* 132.

92. Two books in the Old Testament, Job and Ecclesiastes, focus on the question of why God allows evil and suffering. Other passages that raise the same question are: Exodus 5:22; Numbers 11:11; 14:3; Joshua 7:7–9; Judges 6:13; 21:3; Psalms 10:1; 13:1–2; 22:1–3; 42:3; 44:23–24; 73:2–14; 74:1; 77:7–9; 82:2; 88:14–18; 89:46; 94:3; Isaiah 63:15–17; Jeremiah 12:1; 20:18; Lamentations 5:20–22; Habakkuk 1:2–4; 13; Malachi 3:14–15; Matthew 27:47.

93. Proverbs 19:3.

94. Carl Gustav Jung, MD, *Modern Man in Search of a Soul* (New York: A Harvest/HBJ Book, Harcourt Brace Jovanovich, 1933), 199.

95. *A Life Without Pain,* directed by Melody Gilbert (St. Paul, MN: Frozen Feet Films, 2005). www.alifewithoutpain.com.

96. Dr. Paul Brand and Philip Yancey, *Pain: The Gift Nobody Wants* (New York: HarperCollins Publisher, Zonderman, 1993).

97. Harold S. Kushner, *When Bad Things Happen to Good People* (New York: Schocken Books, 1981). Rabbi Kushner relied on one of the books of poetry in the Old Testament—Job (pronounced to rhyme with "robe"). Job suffered a series of tragedies even though he was a "righteous" man. Most of the book consists of Job's friends speculating about why God had inflicted such calamities on him. But all his friends were wrong to assume God had caused Job's problems. The first few verses make it clear that some other force, not God, had done all those terrible things to Job.
I once saw Rabbi Kushner interviewed about his book. He summed up his position by saying he found it impossible *not* to believe in God, so he had to believe that God is all-loving but not all-powerful or that God is all-powerful but not all-loving. He felt that the former was more likely than the latter.

98. 1 Kings 19:12.

99. Some scholars think this reference to the famous line from *Hamlet* is based on a popular but misguided interpretation of what the character Gertrude actually meant. Nevertheless, it serves my purpose here.

100. Gregg Stebben, *The Pocket Professor, Religion: Everything You Need to Know About Religion*, Denis Boyles, ed. (New York: Pocket Books, 1999), 88–89.

101. Christopher Hitchens, *God Is Not Great*, 195.

102. The Atheist Bus Campaign was created by comedy writer Ariane Sherine to buy advertising space on the sides of public buses in Britain to display the slogan: "There's probably no God. Now stop worrying and enjoy yourself." With financial support from Richard Dawkins and the British Humanist Association, the first bus with the slogan started running on January 6, 2009, and the campaign soon grew to include about eight hundred buses throughout the UK.

103. Richard Dawkins, *The God Delusion*, 51 (paperback, 73).

104. S. T. Joshi, *God's Defenders* (New York: Prometheus Books, 2003), 9–10.

105. William Barclay, *The Daily Study Bible Series: The Gospel of Matthew, Volume 1* (Philadelphia: The Westminister Press, 1975), 97.

106. Bruce Sheiman, *An Atheist Defends Religion*, ix, xv.

107. Carl Gustav Jung, *Modern Man in Search of a Soul*, 229.

108. Matthew 6:6.

109. Matthew 6:9–13.

110. Psalm 46:10.

111. Matthew 7:8.

112. Matthew 7:12.

113. Mahabharata 5:1517.

114. Talmud, Sabbath 31A.

115. http://www.religioustolerance.org. and http://www.teachingvalues.com. Here are some of the ways the Golden Rule

is stated as translated into English:

Christianity: "So in everything, do to others what you would have them do to you, for this sums up the Law and the Prophets" (Jesus, from the Sermon on the Mount, Matthew 7:12).

Islam: "Not one of you truly believes until you wish for others what you wish for yourself" (The Prophet Muhammad, Hadith of Bukhari 2:6). "That which you want for yourself, seek for mankind" (Sukhanan-i-Muhammad, Teheran, 1938 [English Title: Conversations of Muhammad]).

Hinduism: "This is the sum of duty: Do not do to others what would cause pain if done to you" (Mahabharata 5:1517).

Buddhism: "Treat not others in ways that you yourself would find hurtful" (The Buddha, Udana-Varga 5.18). "Consider yourself as others" (Dhammapada 10.1).

Judaism: "What is hateful to you, do not do to others. This is the whole Torah; all the rest is commentary" (Hillel, Talmud, Shabbath 31A).

Confucianism: "Tse-kung asked, 'Is there one word you know that can serve as a principle for conduct for life?' Confucius replied, 'It is the word reciprocity. Do not impose on others what you yourself do not desire'" (Doctrine of the Mean 13.3). "Try your best to treat others as you would wish to be treated yourself" (Confucius, Analects XV.24).

Bahá'í: "Lay not on any soul a load that you would not wish to be laid upon you, and desire not for anyone the things you would not desire for yourself" (Bahá'u'lláh, Gleanings).

116. Christopher Hitchens, *God Is Not Great*, 213–215.

117. Ibid., 213–214.

118. See, for example, Matthew 25:31–46; Luke 14:13–14; Matthew 7:21–23; John 14:15.

119. James 2:14–24.

120. Ephesians 2:8–10.

121. Billy Graham, *Peace With God, Revised and Expanded* (Waco, TX: Word Books, 1984), 113.

122. For an example, see Matt 7:21–23.

123. C. S. Lewis, *Mere Christianity* (San Francisco: HarperSanFrancisco, 1980), 148.

124. Of course the Golden Rule itself leads to worldly charity. But many passages are more specific, such as Matthew 7:21–23; 25:31–46; Luke 14:13–14; John 14:15.

125. "Thank you, Patrick, For Your Applause," *Christian Ethics Today*, Winter 2006 issue, 12.

126. Arthur C. Brooks, *Who Really Cares*, 75–95.

127. Luke 21:1–4.

128. Luke 15:3–6.

129. Luke 10:25–37.

130. Matthew 25:31–46.

131. Matthew 6:15.

132. Jordana Lewis and Jerry Adler, "Forgive and Let Live," *Newsweek* magazine, September 27, 2004, p. 52.

133. Everett L. Worthington Jr., *The Power of Forgiving* (Dowers Grove, IL: Templeton Foundation Press, 2005).

134. As quoted in "Forgive and Let Live," *Newsweek* magazine. See note 132 above.

135. Matthew 22:39, quoting Leviticus 19:18.

136. Peter Drucker, Foreword to Bob Buford, *Halftime* (Grand Rapids, MI: Zondervan, 1994), 15.

137. Many books based on extensive evidence show that people of faith and charity tend to be happier than anyone else. Ironically, one of the best is Bruce Sheiman's *An Atheist Defends Religion*. Another book that compresses the findings of many studies into very brief "entries" is Grenville-Cleave and Ilona Boniwell's *The Happiness Equation*. See entry 94 (127) and entry 96 (129). *See also* Arthur C. Brooks, *Who Really Cares*, 137–160; and David G. Myers, PhD, *The Pursuit of Happiness* (New York: Avon Books, 1992).

138. Richard Dawkins, *The God Delusion*, 50 (paperback, 73). For the full quote, see M. Scott Peck, *Further Along the Road Less Traveled* (New York: Simon & Schuster, 1993), 174.

139. Philippians 4:7.

140. C. S. Lewis, *Mere Christianity* (San Francisco: HarperSanFrancisco, 2001), 146.

141. Matthew 7:7–8.

142. Deuteronomy 4:29.

143. Carl Gustav Jung, MD, *Psychology & Religion*, 113–114.

144. When I began the faith experiment I was vaguely aware of the fact that at least a few intellectuals had, since the first century, discussed the question of who Jesus claimed to be: God, the Son of God, the "Son of Man," or all of the above? I made no effort to sort all that out. For the purpose of the experiment I just assumed Jesus was in some way divine.

145. Huston Smith, *The World's Religions* (San Francisco: HarperSanFrancisco, 1991), 36.

146. Some scholars say the Buddha may have been an atheist. I'm no expert on Buddhism, but I am not convinced the Buddha was an atheist. He never said there is no God; he just refused to discuss it. But he was born into a religion that believed in nearly two million gods. It's my impression that he didn't want to open the theological floodgates to questions about the nature or number of gods. He felt that would drown out thoughts on how best to live our lives. That sort of thing has certainly happened among some Christian intellectuals, dating back to the first century. They argued incessantly about what God was like, both physically and spiritually. Some of them enforced their views *about* God in a way that flagrantly violated the laws *of* God, including the one Jesus said summed up all the others—the Golden Rule.

147. Smith's reference to an "average mind" was in the original version of his book *The Religions of Man* (New York: Harper Colophon Books, 1958), 178. He changed that wording in his revised edition, *The World's Religions*, perhaps to avoid insulting people like me with an "average" mind.

148. *The World Book Encyclopedia of 1972*, s.v. "Judaism," 144. "Judaism accepts converts, but does not seek them."

149. Will Durant, *The Story of Civilization Vol. 3, Caesar and Christ* (New York: Simon and Schuster, 1944), 652.

150. Vincent Carroll & David Shiflett, *Christianity on Trial: Arguments Against Anti-Religious Bigotry*, 140–141.

151. Vincent Carroll and David Shiflett, *Christianity on Trial*.

152. Timothy George, "Is Christ Divided?," *Christianity Today*, July 2005, 31. For a more current estimate, look under "denominationalism" in the *Oxford World Encyclopedia*. History books tend to focus on three major schisms: (1) The Great Schism of 1054 that separated the Western Roman Catholic Church from the Eastern Orthodox Church, (2) The Protestant Reformation (or Rebellion) that began in 1517 when Martin Luther tried to reform the Roman Catholic Church, and (3) The Old Believers Schism in 1666 that produced the Russian Orthodox Church.

153. A few passages in red letters may not be the words of Jesus. For example, some interpreters do not regard John 3:16–21 as quotations of Jesus, but as comments made by the author of that Gospel.

154. Robert W. Funk, *Honest to Jesus* (San Francisco: HarperSanFrancisco, 1996), 8n.

155. Albert Schweitzer, *Out of My Life and Thought* (New York: A Mentor Book, 1959), 48.

156. Schweitzer, *The Quest of the Historical Jesus* (Baltimore: The Johns Hopkins University Press, 1998), 183.

157. Ibid., 400.

158. Matthew 7:12; 22:35–40.

159. Matthew 7:28–29.

160. John 2:13–16; Matthew 23:13–36 (got angry); John 11:33 (sad and troubled); John 19:28 (thirsty); John 4:6 (tired); Luke 8:23 (slept).

161. John 11:35.

162. Luke 5:16.

163. Matthew 27:46.

164. M. Scott Peck, MD, *Further Along the Road Less Traveled* (New York: Simon & Schuster, 1993), 160.

165. Will Durant, *The Story of Civilization Vol. 3, Caeser and Christ*, 557.

166. Matthew 7:13–14, 21–23.

167. Elton Trueblood, *A Place to Stand* (San Francisco: Harper & Row, 1969), 58.

168. William Barclay, *The Daily Study Bible Series, Revised Edition, The Letters to Timothy, Titus, and Philemon* (Philadelphia: The Westminister Press, 1975), 229.

169. Christine Wicker, "True Believers," *Dallas Morning News,* August 23, 1987.

170. Matthew 19:14. He also said, "I tell you the truth, unless you change and become like little children, you will never enter the kingdom of heaven" (Matthew 18:3).

171. With one exception these figures are taken from John Riches, *The Bible: A Very Short Introduction* (New York: Oxford University Press, 2000), 3. The exception is the total number of languages in the world, which that book says is 6,500. According to the Living Tongues Institute for Endangered Languages, the total estimate of documented languages has risen to 6,910, including the language called Koro that was discovered in 2010 in a remote corner of India.

172. Jeffrey Weiss, "What America Believes," *Dallas Morning News,* June 24, 2008, 1A, 10A. The survey of more than thirty-six thousand people was done by the Pew Forum for Religion & Public Life and released on June 23, 2008.

173. Catechism of the Catholic Church, n 847.

174. John 14:6.

175. Acts 4:12.

176. Romans 2:13-16.

177. James Denison, *Wrestling with God* (Carol Stream, IL: Saltriver, 2008), 158.

178. Some who believe in the exclusivity doctrine ask a legitimate question: If people who never hear the Gospel can go to heaven anyway, why did Jesus tell his disciples to tell it to others? Perhaps the answer is found in the question. The word "gospel" means good news. The good news is that one can receive God's grace and forgiveness even if they don't deserve it. That is exceedingly good news to people brought up to believe in angry gods. Moreover, people who knowingly follow the teachings of Jesus practice more humanitarian charity than those who don't.

So sharing the written Gospel makes the world a better place—
and that's reason enough to share it.

179. Matthew 7:8.

180. *Eerdmans Dictionary of the Bible* (Grand Rapids, MI:
William B. Eerdmans Publishing Company, 2000), 573. *See
also* s.v. "GEHENNA," 489. Some believe that people who
go to hell will be punished and then die. So their suffering
will end, along with their very existence. Those who hold
this view say hell is an "everlasting" punishment only in the
sense that death is everlasting. This view is based on various
passages in the Bible, including several statements by Jesus.
For example, he indicated that both body *and soul* can be
"destroyed" in hell (Matt. 10:28) and that those who go there
will "perish" (John 3:16).

181. Rob Bell, *Love Wins* (New York: HarperOne, 2011); Charles
Gillihan, *Hell No! A Fundamentalist Preacher Rejects Eternal
Torment* (Westbrook, CT: Praeger Publishers, 2011); Pentecostal
Bishop Carlton Pearson, *The Gospel of Inclusion* (New York:
Atria Books, 2008). *See also* Jon Meachum, "Is Hell Dead?,"
Time, April 25, 2011, 38–43.

182. Bart D. Ehrman, *From Jesus to Constantine: A History of Early
Christianity, Part I* (Chantilly, VA: The Teaching Company,
2004), 62–63. Emphasis added.

183. Will Durant, *The Story of Civilization Vol. 3, Caesar and Christ*,
652.

184. Ibid.

185. J. B. Phillips, *Ring of Truth* (Wheaton, IL: Harold Shaw
Publishers, 1977), 79.

186. The Fellowship of Christians in Science, http://www.asa3.org.

187. Lee Strobel set out to disprove the Bible when he was an
atheist. He investigated from his perspectives as a lawyer and
journalist. But he became convinced the Bible is true. See *The
Case for Christ* (Zondervan Publishing House, 1998) and *The
Case for Faith* (Grand Rapids, MI: Zondervan Publishing
House, 2000). He names other skeptics who have found faith in
a similar way.

188. Exodus 20:14.

189. Will Durant, *The Story of Civilization Vol. 3, Caesar and Christ*, 652.

190. William Barclay, The Daily Study Bible Series, *The Gospel of Mathew, Revised Edition, Volume 1* (Philadelphia: The Westminister Press, 1975), 320–321.

191. Helen Keller, *The Story of My Life* (New York: Tess Press), 112–113.

192. Albert Schweitzer, *Out of My Life and Thought*, 92.

193. Ibid., 92–93.

194. Richard Dawkins, *The God Delusion*, 306 (paperback, 346).

195. Ibid., 51 (paperback, 73).

196. Ibid., 5–6 (paperback, 28).

197. Ibid., 5–6, 306 (paperback, 28, 346).

198. Ibid., 5–6 (paperback, 28).

199. Ibid., 51 (paperback, 73).

200. *The American Journal of Psychiatry*, as quoted on the back cover of the paperback edition of Victor E. Frankl, *Man's Search for Meaning* (New York: Washington Square Press, 1959).

201. Viktor E. Frankl, MD, PhD, *Man's Search for Meaning*, 4th ed. (Boston: Beacon Press, 1992), 104.

202. Ibid.

203. Ibid., 105.

204. Ibid., 117.

205. Ibid., 110.

206. Ibid., 142.

207. Arthur C. Brooks, *Who Really Cares*, 137–160; Allen Luks with Peggy Payne, *The Healing Power of Doing Good: The Health and Spiritual Benefits of Helping Others* (New York: Fawcett Columbine, 1991); David G. Myers, PhD, *The Pursuit of Happiness* (New York: Avon Books, 1992); Martin E.P. Seligman, PhD, *Authentic Happiness* (New York: Free Press, 2002).

208. Arthur C. Brooks, *Who Really Cares*, 137–160; Grenville-Cleave and Ilona Boniwell, *The Happiness Equation*, entry 96, page 129.

209. "British atheists roll out ad campaign," *The Dallas Morning News*, January 7, 2009, 6A.

210. Antony Flew, *There Is a God*, 156–157.

211. Richard Dawkins, "Preface to the Paperback Edition, *The God Delusion*, 19.

About the Author

John Scott, JD, began his working life as a teenager in the Texas oil fields. Then he entered law school, where he became president of the student bar association and editor of the *Law Review*. He began his legal career as a litigator and retired forty years later as the senior vice president and general counsel of an international corporation. "Being a skeptic served me well professionally," he says, "because no client wants to be represented by a gullible lawyer. But at a personal level it led to the collapse of my religious faith. While reading countless books on the God debate I came across a few suggestions that led me back to faith and a profoundly better life." Scott and his wife, Joan, reside in Dallas, Texas, where they do volunteer work. He teaches leadership at a local university.